Three Journeys in the Levant

CW00498002

SHUSHA GUPPY was born and raise
Paris. Her previous books include *The Blindfold Horse*, *A Girl in Paris* and *Looking Back*. She is the London editor of the celebrated American literary journal *The Paris Review* and contributes to publications on both sides of the Atlantic. She has won several prizes, the last in 1996 for the French edition of her first book, *Un Jardin à Téhéran*. She lives in London.

The cover of this book reproduces a photograph of a ceramic vase made by **CAROLINDA TOLSTOY**.

The illustrations to be found facing the title page and pages 1, 35 & 85 are by the artist and writer **JESSICA DOUGLAS-HOME**.

تقدیم به مادر، خانم هنیه اکبر

با بهترین آرزوها .

THREE JOURNEYS

in the LEVANT

شرکت چاپی - بهار

SHUSHA GUPPY

Starhaven

ISBN 0-936315-17-2

STARHAVEN
42 Frognal, London NW3 6AG
Tel: 020 7435 8724 Fax: 020 7435 4169
In US, c/o Box 2573, La Jolla, CA 92038, USA
Email: starhaven@aesthesia.co.uk

Typeset in Ehrhardt by John Mallinson
Printed & bound by CPI Copyspeed, 38 Ballard's Lane, London N3 2BJ

CONTENTS

ACKNOWLEDGEMENTS

I wish to express my deep gratitude to Patrick Leigh-Fermor for reading and correcting my manuscript. He has been my model and inspiration ever since I first read *The Traveller's Tree*. He returned the script with meticulous corrections, comments and advice. I am honoured that this book has passed through his hand.

My thanks also to Joan Leigh-Fermor for her great kindness and support over the years.

These journeys began in the later 1990s as travel pieces for *Vogue*, *The Times* and *Harper's & Queen*, and I wish to thank them for the assignments and for their practical help; also my friend Marc Trillard for his encouragement and publication of an earlier version of the Jordan chapter as 'À la découverte d'une terre chargée d'histoire' in his *Nouvelles du monde* series for Collection Afat Voyages.

Since these pieces were written, Israel has pulled out of South Lebanon and King Hussein of Jordan and President Hafez Assad of Syria have died and been succeeded by their sons.

Transliteration: Except for Arabic words that have entered the English dictionary or common usage, I have used simple English phonetic spellings.

FOREWORD

I have nothing but praise for Shusha Guppy's excellent book on the Levant, and the praise is all the higher as I was at first apprehensive. I feared that it might belong to a category that I usually avoid like the plague, books that seem to knock the mystery and adventure out of the countries they cover, making them, somehow, seem trodden and stale in advance.

Looking at the book, and spotting Shelley's 'Ozymandias' quotation I had a flicker of hope. Seeing the author's name, the flicker became a heartening flame: her fascinating book *The Blindfold Horse*, about her family in Persia and her growing up there, came immediately to mind. Rooted for many years in England, she is devoted to history, literature and travel, especially in the Levant, and trilingual in English, French and her native Persian. Her insights into the Near East, and her study of the records of Western travellers who have preceded her, have qualified her to observe and evaluate them, and to select the passages that will most interest a less-learned traveller. Her facility with history, art, religions and poetry of those ancient regions enables her to transmit her reactions to the splendours that surround a newcomer. Politics and wars have left many scars, and they play an unavoidable part in these pages. Shusha Guppy deals with them with balanced and unpartisan clarity. But in the end it is the traveller's fascination with the wonders of past ages that emerges with the most vigour, and these, and many other delights, are presented to us with a captivating informality.

– Patrick Leigh-Fermor

JORDAN
Through an Antique Land

I met a traveller from an antique land
Who said: Two vast and trunkless legs of stone
Stand in the desert. Near them, on the sand,
Half sunk, a shattered visage lies, whose frown
And wrinkled lip, and sneer of cold command,
Tell that its sculptor well those passions read
Which yet survive, stamped on these lifeless things,
The hand that mocked them and the heart that fed;
And on the pedestal these words appear:
'My name is Ozymandias, king of kings:
Look on my works, ye Mighty, and despair!'
Nothing beside remains. Round the decay
Of that colossal wreck, boundless and bare
The lone and level sands stretch far away.

— Percy Bysshe Shelley, 'Ozymandias'

The dapper young man at Reception in the Grand Hotel in Amman seemed straight out of central casting: an Omar Sharif, with dark tender eyes, shiny black air and suave manners. 'Welcome to Jordan!' he smiled.

I explained that in the rush of departure from London, I had left my watch behind, and might the hotel be kind enough to lend me a small clock? 'Have my watch please,' he said and

1

promptly took it off his wrist. No amount of protestation would prevail. So for the next week I travelled through Jordan sporting a huge, loose gold watch. My benefactor's name was Rahim ('Most Kind'), which appears in the first verse of the Holy Koran as God's foremost attribute; and his spontaneous gesture made me feel very welcome and at home.

I had last been in the Middle East in 1977, in Persia, two years before the revolution that toppled the Shah and brought Ayatollah Khomeini to power. In the years that followed, Persia was ravaged by its long war with neighbouring Iraq, and the whole region was plunged into an inferno of violence. My family and home were destroyed, and there seemed to be nothing left to which I might want to return. Yet I was still nostalgically drawn back to the region. I am not alone in this, for the Middle East casts a peculiar spell. Here was our original abode, the Garden from which we had been banished and to which we longed to return. Or is it the barrenness and purity of the desert in contrast to our own cluttered world which draws us, or simply the warmth and generosity and idiosyncrasy of the people? Or could it be that the birthplace of the three mono-theistic religions touches a chord in the psyche? Since Persia was closed to me, I chose Jordan to travel to first, the safest and gentlest country in the region.

Before setting off, I sought to acquaint myself with the Hashemite Kingdom through maps and guides and travellers' tales. Modern Jordan emerged from the splinters of the Ottoman Empire in 1920 and for three decades remained a British protectorate, achieving full independence only in 1953 after the accession of King Hussein. On the map the country looks like an odd pattern of cracks on a piece of china, surrounded by similar jagged shapes – to the north Syria and Lebanon, to the west Israel, to the east Iraq, to the south Saudi Arabia. That it has survived, despite scanty resources, amid the cataclysms raging among its rich and powerful neighbours is largely due to the genuine popularity and political skill and intuition of King Hussein.

Jordan is very small – the size of Portugal – but varied in climate and scenery. It is strewn with antiquities, most of which have only recently been rescued from centuries of sand and oblivion – no less than four Roman amphitheatres have been dug out in the last few decades, one of which is at the centre of Amman, the capital city. In the past, caravans of merchants and travellers to the Holy Land spent weeks crossing the desert. Today a network of good roads criss-crosses the country and brings the grand sites within reach of one-day journeys from Amman, and foreign visitors have become Jordan's second largest source of income. Even so, years could be spent exploring it thoroughly, as many archaeologists and anthropologists do. Modern travellers with only a few days to spare can choose among various interesting alternatives.

While a companion provides a sense of security and the pleasure of sharing, I prefer to wander on my own, at least on first visits, and trust to chance encounters and beginner's luck. Local transport, however uncomfortable, is the best way of getting to know a country and its people but may involve unforeseen hazards – breakdown, cancellations and delays. I had limited time, and hiring a car with a driver seemed wisest.

Gibril, my driver and guide, met me at the airport. His name could not have been more reassuring: Gibril is the Arabic for Gabriel, the Archangel who appeared to the Prophet Mohammad in his mountain retreat and brought him the credo of Islam, 'There is no god except God and Mohammad is his Rasul', and thereafter guided him through his mission of revealing the Sacred Book to the world.

My Gibril at first seemed rather diffident; he volunteered no information about himself and expressed no opinions. But during our travel he relaxed, and although he spoke little English and I knew even less Arabic, we understood each other; he had a subtle sense of humour tinged with the skepticism of those to whom much has been promised but little delivered. When our journey ended, he apologised for his broken English; I reassured him by quoting Rumi, 'It is better to be of the same heart than of the same tongue.' He wrote it down in Arabic. 'I keep this in memory of you,' he said.

The gentle and knowledgeable Gibril was 42, but he looked years older. He was thin and hollow-cheeked, but his sad black eyes came alight when his interest was aroused. His hair had the dullness of smoke, and years of chain-smoking had done for his teeth, which were either black or missing. 'Why do you smoke so much?' I asked. He had a wife and several children, and his driver's salary was hardly sufficient to keep them; how could he burn up his hard-earned cash like this, and destroy his lungs in the process?

'We Arabs visit each other a lot, and everywhere – in shops, houses and cafés – we drink a little cup of tea. It makes nervous, so we smoke to calm our nerves,' he explained, lighting another cigarette. 'But I try to cut down, and I successful, until last week… terrible… terrible.' He shook his head and his eyes clouded with tears. What had happened, I wondered. He waited a moment to recover his composure, then told me:

He had four children ranging in age from three to twelve. A few days before my arrival, the older ones were at school and the youngest, a girl, was at home playing in the yard. Her mother went to the next door neighbour on some errand and lingered over a cup of tea. Meanwhile, the child put her head inside a bucket of water to drink and got stuck. She must have struggled and tried to shout, but the water stifled her, and she drowned. When the mother found her a few minutes later, she screamed for help; the neighbours rushed in from everywhere and took the child to the hospital. Everything was done to resuscitate her, but she was gone... They had buried her the day I arrived.

The horror of the story left me speechless. I visualised a sweet little girl flitting about in the courtyard, feeling hot and thirsty, finding the pail of drinking water... I had seen children play barefoot in the desert and had worried about deadly snakes and scorpions. But water? Our most precious ally in a land of sand and rock? The cruel irony was not lost on Gibril – his face was bathed in tears, and his shoulders were shuddering with silent sobs.

'I punished my wife. I did...' he said. I said that his wife's sorrow, being compounded by guilt, must be even more acute, and quoted the *hadith*: 'You should not strike a woman even with a flower.' He said that he had never lifted a finger on her before: 'But I couldn't help myself – she shouldn't have left the child alone.'

I was surprised that he was working so soon after the tragedy. 'What can I do? The others need bread.' The logic was disarming.

Twice since the World War II the population of Jordan has doubled, almost overnight, largely with Palestinian refugees. The first time was in 1948, when the State of Israel was brought into being, the second was after the Six Day War in 1967. Today over 40% of Jordanians are of Palestinian origin, and the country's birthrate is high. In spite of considerable foreign aid and steady development, most of the people are very poor. Gibril could not afford to take any time off to mourn his daughter. I offered to pay his wages and find another driver, so that he could go home and be with his family, but he declined. 'No. It is better I work. I talk with you and forget a little.'

And so began our journey across his antique land.

'If you know two people in the Middle East, you'll know everybody,' said a London friend who knew the region well, and before I left he gave me the telephone numbers of an Iraqi lady living in exile (I shall call her Leyla) and of Ali Jabri, a painter and designer famous throughout the Arab world. 'There is a fair amount to see in Amman,' Ali Jabri told me when I rang him, and he kindly offered to take me sightseeing. I had struck lucky: with his knowledge of art and archaeology, his charm and sense of humour, he turned out to be the best of guides and an ideal companion.

When I saw him the next morning in the foyer of the hotel, I was surprised. I had expected him to be dark and of medium height, like most men I had met in the Middle East. Instead I found a handsome 'Englishman' – tall and slim, with blond hair and blue eyes, like a young Prince Philip, an impression enhanced by his accent. Thanks to him and his friends, and Gibril with his companions, I learnt much about Jordan from different points of view in the week that I spent there.

Ali owed his European looks to his Circassian ancestry. Two hundred and fifty thousand of Jordan's five million population are descendants of the Caucasian immigrants who fled the persecution of Russia in the 19th Century and settled in an area of the Ottoman Empire covering present-day Syria, Lebanon, Palestine and Jordan. The majority were Circassians, and there was among them a smaller group of Chechens and Armenians. Circassian women were famous for their beauty and prized as slaves, concubines and wives. With time these minorities were absorbed into the native population and passed on their white skin and blue or green eyes to their descendants.

When it became the capital of newly created Jordan in 1920, Amman was a small Ottoman town of a few thousand inhabitants, with a long history, a little bazaar and a mosque. Today these comprise the downtown of a vast metropolis that sprawls over seven hills and holds a third of the country's five million population. Three thousand years ago Amman was called Rabath Ammon. In the Old Testament it was where King David sent Uriah the Hittite to his death because of his designs on his beautiful wife Bathsheba. Amman was renamed Philadelphia by the Egyptians, after Ptolemy Philadelphus who conquered it. Greeks, Persians and Romans followed, before Islam swept through the region in 630 AD. The town flourished briefly under the Umayyads in the 8th Century, then went into decline. All over Jordan vestiges of this long and rich past remain, many rescued by recent excavations from layers of sand and rubble.

In Amman, the most famous vestige is the citadel, an ancient fortress on top of the highest hill, with a superb view over the whole city and the desert beyond. Successive conquerors who used the citadel's strategic position have left their monuments: a Greek acropolis, a temple of Hercules built by Marcus Aurelius in 162 AD, a Byzantine church and al-Qasr, a castle of the Umayyads.

Large scale excavation and restoration works are going on, and walking among the ruins is like treading through a vast building site – with cranes and cables and scaffolding and mounds of stone. It is also a journey through time and an exercise for the imagination.

Part of the original Iron Age wall that surrounded the hill is still exposed in the northeast corner, and from there you move forward through successive periods. A $6,000,000 project will eventually restore the Temple of Hercules to its former glory; beside it once stood a gigantic statue of the god, thought, from a surviving piece of elbow and a foot, to have been thirty feet high. Al-Qasr, the square building in the middle, was originally a Roman palace which the Umayyads rebuilt and decorated, and remains of fine carvings on the walls show how splendid it must have been.

Despite its size, the small nearby Museum of Archaeology has some fine pieces: pottery, jewellery, weapons, cult objects and items dating from immemorial times to the Islamic period. Ali pointed to a three thousand year old skull showing traces of surgery: 'You see here that the patient was operated upon twice and survived – but died the third time.' He pointed out places where the bone had been drilled. 'This is a replica, the original is in the British Museum.' There was a baby preserved for thousands of years: 'They used to put their dead children in jars and bury them under the sitting-room floor, to keep them close to the family.'

From the highest point of the citadel, Ali pointed out some landmarks. The slender minarets of the 19th Century al-Darvish Mosque, the city's grandest, rose among flat-roofed buildings; to the left stood the King's Palace, surrounded by gardens bordered with cypress trees.

'In Roman times monumental stairways went down from the citadel to the old agora, the forum and the amphitheatre in the centre of the town below,' Ali said. 'Now we have to drive by a twisting road through the traffic.'

We wound downhill to the Roman complex: 'Until recently a river ran through the middle, bordered with trees and gardens; it was a sylvan scene. Opposite the amphitheatre was Grand Hotel Philadelphia, where T. E. Lawrence and other Western travellers used to stay. Then the river was blocked, the hotel was replaced by shops and ice-cream stalls, and the town expanded outwardly with residential areas moving further and further out and leaving the centre to decay.'

A five thousand seat amphitheatre, built on a slope to catch the sun at a right angle, is still used for concerts and open-air events. On either side, the vaulted corridors of its entrance and exit have been turned into Museums of Popular Tradition and Folklore. This was done by Ali Jabri's aunt, Seyyedah Wasfi, then the Prime Minister's wife, in the early 1980s, and Ali was put in charge of the installations and displays. The magnificent collection of costumes in the Museum of Popular Tradition dates back to the Crusaders. Gold and silver jewellery, embroidered clothes and headgear, domestic utensils and saddle-bags, displayed with great discrimination, give a sense of daily life in towns as well as tents in the desert. The whole of the Arab Middle East was once linked together, while ethnic differences showed in the details. Ali explained: 'The colours and patterns of the embroidery indicate a woman's tribe or her village, her social position and rank, whether she was rich or poor, married or a virgin, a wife or a widow. A young man looking for a bride would study her embroidery to get an idea of her level of refinement.'

I told him that the romantic in me lamented the passing of the Bedouins' pastoral world, as inevitably the values by which they lived – honour, hospitality, generosity, chivalry – would gradually disappear too. 'It was not an easy life, particularly for the women, who had to deal with the practical side of things. Modern Bedouin girls don't want to live in tents and weave cloth,' said Ali. 'They want to go to school, dance in discos and choose their own husbands. Who can blame them?'

Not I, who had run away from another traditional society whose passing I now mourned.

The Folklore Museum opposite shows traditional living in Jordan: a Bedouin family in its tent, a decorated camel and its rider – perhaps a bridegroom – musical instruments, weaving and cooking gear. In the museum's shop and in the bazaar, one can buy reproductions of old silver and turquoise; jewellery and embroidered clothes.

I was fascinated by the Romans' method of handling crowds: spectators entered by one covered stone passage and left by another on the opposite side, so that there was no rush or scuffle. Similarly they regulated the supply of water by managing the overflow of the river with a network of underground conduits and channels. They laid down paved streets and colonnades, a forum and a shrine to the nymphs, thus creating a Rome in miniature on the edge of the Arabian Desert. No wonder the legions are said to have felt at home here.

Other Roman buildings have recently been discovered near the amphitheatre: an odeum – a small theatre for musical shows – and a nymphaeum, the town's central fountain, whose decorative facade has survived intact. Hidden amid the urban sprawl they can easily be missed.

Next, through a maze of streets choked with traffic and teeming with a variegated crowd of shoppers and vendors, we leapt across the centuries from ancient Rome to the bazaar built in 19th Century Ottoman times. In Middle Eastern bazaars, merchants selling the same goods cluster together: the goldsmiths, the drapers and the potters each have their section. There are no big stores where shopping is an impersonal business; everything here depends on personal contact and charm and trust, and shopping can be a delight. The gold souk sparkled with rows upon rows of bangles strung up behind window panes, and the necklaces and rings on display catch the sun and twinkle seductively. Ali knew some of the shopkeepers: 'Ahlan-wa-sahlan!' they said, inviting us in and offering us cups of tea and coffee, which seemed to appear by magic. There is not much haggling, but one has to observe certain courtesies: 'Take it, it is yours, you need not pay at all,' they say, if you question their first quoted price. I finally bought a present – a little gold 'Fatimah's Hand' (named after the Prophet's daughter, but among the Christians called 'Mary's Hand'). It is really a pagan amulet predating monotheism, but it is a pretty keepsake to bring skill at untangling the knots of life. At a draper's, we went through the same pleasant rites before leaving with a little embroidered bolero for a child.

My goldsmith did not have a credit-card machine and gave my card to a young man to take to a friend's shop to use his. After a while, when he had not returned, a note of worry must have crept into my voice, for the shopkeeper frowned, saying, 'Rest assured, lady, nothing will happen to it'. And indeed the young man came in at that moment. Later I told Ali that in Europe credit card theft and signature forgery were routine. 'It can't happen in a bazaar, where everyone knows everyone else. A dishonest merchant would be shamed out of business.' Shame is indeed a social regulator. In our societies where individual freedom seems to have no limit, shame is not a deterrent – when anything goes, there is a danger that everything goes – but here it is still potent.

As we moved through the streets, Ali pointed to some beautiful Ottoman buildings. 'These are architectural jewels at the very heart of the city, yet they let them fall to bits. Look at those elegant proportions, those lovely wrought-iron balconies and slim columns! Look at those neon lights and flashy signs across their facades! We have started a campaign for saving old buildings, but unlike Roman and Byzantine ruins these ones don't draw tourism. We need something like English Heritage. The Department of Antiquities takes care of ancient buildings, but the Ottoman period is not considered old enough! The city centre should become a pedestrian zone; motor traffic should be sorted out, and old buildings restored. The dark age of the 1960s has descended on us – as if Georges Pompidou had had his way in Paris, with plans for underground parking beneath Notre Dame! And there isn't much time left – as the years go by the process of decay becomes irreversible. Yet these buildings are the repository of nostalgia, the locus of the collective memory. Above all, the renovation of these old houses could start the revival of a native domestic architecture.'

I recognised in Ali's tone the same mixture of exasperation, anger and despair at official short-sightedness and the philistinism encountered all over the Third World. I remembered how similar beautiful houses were gradually pulled down in my district in Teheran to be replaced by hideous American 1950s-style tract 'villas' and European municipal housing, until only two houses were left – ours and the Grand Mullah of Teheran's, museum pieces that were destroyed by 'developers' after the revolution of 1979. But those houses indicated that, until the beginning of this century, there had been a distinct native architecture which combined comfort with beauty and was in tune with the climate and the culture of the country.

We had lunch at the Hotel Intercontinental – today's version of the old Philadelphia and the headquarters of foreign journalists and visiting dignitaries. Its large café is the rendezvous of Amman's intelligentsia, and its art gallery, where Ali and other famous artists give regular exhibitions, is well-known in the Arab world. The self-service buffet was sumptuous: the best of Lebanese cuisine with Jordanian specialities and Western dishes.

After lunch we met friends of Ali's in the café and settled down to a long discussion about the state of the world, the Middle East, the dizzy waltz of alliances and enmities between different countries, their relations with the West, in particular America... It reminded me of my student days in Paris; in England there is no café life, and politics don't arouse the same passions.

That evening we joined Leyla for dinner at Romero's, a small restaurant in a leafy residential area not far from the Intercontinental. Its cuisine is Franco-Italian, with a few local dishes, and its attractive décor is similar to that of a trattoria. Its congenial atmosphere draws a cosmopolitan clientele of Arab and European visitors. The King and Queen are supposed to drop in from time to time.

Leyla belonged to an old, patrician family and was a well-known educationalist when she left Iraq for a life of exile in Jordan. I asked her about her family in Iraq. So afraid was she for their fate that she instinctively looked round and lowered her voice, as if Saddam's spies lurked in all corners. The atmosphere of fear, insecurity and misery she described was similar to what we know of the 1930s in Stalinist Russia: arbitrary arrests, torture, periodic purges of the ruling military clique and all the rest. She did not belong to any resistance movement either within Iraq or abroad, fearing Saddam's revenge upon her family, but she blamed the Americans for leaving him in power after the Gulf War: 'All they had to do was to make his removal a condition of peace, and it would have been done. Instead they listened to the Saudis and feared Iran, and let Saddam go on torturing and killing the Iraqi people.'

It is difficult for a Westerner to understand the resentment of people like Leyla towards the West, in particular America. To say, as I did, that 'the West had no mandate from the United Nations to interfere in Iraq's internal affairs' provokes bitter guffaws of disbelief. The perception is that such 'legalism' is a cynical front, that America only cares about its own interests and doesn't give two hoots what happens to human beings in the Third World. She quoted the American journalist who wrote that, if Kuwait had produced carrots instead of petrol, the West would not have cared who invaded it. There is simply no way of reconciling the perception of people like Leyla with the declared policies of the United States – they *know* the reality. In the circumstances, exile for the lucky few seemed the only choice, Leyla believed.

Ali's was another form of exile: born and brought up in Lebanon, he was sent at the age of seven to Rugby, the English public school, by his anglophile father, and then to Cambridge. Desperately homesick at first, he had gradually adapted to his new environment and, his blond looks helping, had almost become an Englishman. But that early deprivation and sorrow had left an indelible scar in his soul, which explained a touch of melancholy and deep loneliness under his apparent insouciance and biting wit.

Ali had returned to Beirut and become a famous artist when the civil war there had broken out, and he too had chosen Jordan as the nearest safe haven to his lost home. But he felt he belonged to nowhere, except that he missed England, and tried to visit it every year: 'As soon as I arrive at London Airport I feel at peace – I'm home,' he said, 'even if the porter is a turbaned Sikh and the cleaner is a West Indian mama. But after a while I realise I don't fit in – my friends have their own lives, we have drifted apart, I'm not an Englishman, and I don't have a home.'

I told him I knew what he meant, that I had the same feeling whenever I went back to Persia before the revolution – I had gone 'home'; I slept in the same bed in the same room; I was with people I loved. Yet I knew I no longer belonged there (if I ever had), that my friends and relatives had led different lives from mine and that only my parents and our family house provided me with some moorings. Once they were gone, I would be adrift.

Yet does not this feeling of exclusion, of non-belonging, have its advantages, I wondered? Does it not produce a certain awareness – a *lucidité*, as we used to call it in my French youth – of our essential human condition?

It certainly provides a different vision – what the Greek author Nikos Kazantzakis called 'the Cretan Eye': one that sees both East and West. 'We are all exiles, Ali,' I ventured, 'and we sometimes envy those who are deeply rooted in their own soil for their sense of security and confidence. But is it real? And is it as desirable as we think? Weren't the spectators at the Nuremberg rallies rooted? Or crazed crowds of revolutionaries and civil warriors and ethnic cleansers all over the world? Aren't we lucky that our alienation and loneliness keep our hands clean of innocent blood? In truth, I would not wish to change my state, nor, I suspect, would you.'

Next day Gibril collected me early, and we set off for Jerash. It is the most complete Roman city in the world. Thirty miles north of Amman, Jerash was discovered in 1806 by Ulrich Seetzen, a German traveller who almost stumbled on it. It was left untouched until 1925 when, under British mandate, restoration began. Dry desert sand is a powerful protector and, as layer after layer was removed, the city emerged in amazingly fine condition. Since then diggings and restorations have laid it bare in its ancient glory.

'We make a little turn to Zarqa,' Gibril informed me as the road forked. Built on the river Zarqa – Jabbok of the Bible – this was once a small Circassian village and had been the head-quarters of the Arab Legion. Today a pipeline brings crude oil here from Iraq. Besides the oil refinery there is a bustling traffic of goods to and from Iraq, so dense that it needed all Gibril's cool head and skill to weave a way through heavy lorries, buses, motorcycles and pedestrians.

Mounds of fruit and vegetables covered the pavements; bananas hung from shop doorways; bolts of gaudy fabrics with gold and silver threads glittered in the sun; barbers shaved and snipped; foodstalls grilled skewers of kebab. I bought some tangerines from the first crop in the Jordan Valley. They were as sweet as lumps of sugar. To the east of Zarqa, the desert stretches to infinity on a smooth sweep of fawn watered-silk, sundered by two shiny ribbons. One goes to Iraq, the other turns south to Saudi Arabia.

We headed north towards Jerash, into quite different scenery – green, with houses and trees and flowers everywhere. Women and children sell fruit and pots from trestle-tables on the edge of the road. The pottery, following the shape of antique water-jugs, is plain or glazed in turquoise, green, lapis lazuli and ochre. Oleanders, jasmines and roses, grown in petrol cans, decorate the thresholds. A little girl combs her hair in a door-way, and children run after the car and wave.

Finally, we reach Jerash. As one approaches the site, Hadrian's Arch, the triple gateway, built in 129 AD to celebrate the Emperor's arrival, looms in the distance like an optical illusion. Gradually the whole city spreads before you as far as the horizon, as if it had been abandoned yesterday.

Jerash was built in 332 BC by Alexander the Great's soldiers in an area that is thought to have been inhabited as far back as Neolithic times. Pompey the Great conquered it in 63 BC and founded the Decapolis, a trading league of ten cities, of which Jerash was one. Soon trade was established with the Nab-ataeans, a native Semitic tribe whose capital was at Petra; and in the following two centuries, Jerash became very rich, reaching its apogee in the 3rd Century. After that, it gradually went into a decline, largely because improved sea routes shifted trade away from the inhospitable desert caravan routes. By the 5th Century, Christianity had become the most important religion in the area, and many churches were built with stones taken from earlier pagan temples. Then, in 614, Persia briefly conquered the region, before everything was swept away by the Muslim invasion in 636, and all that remained of Jerash as a living city was destroyed by an earthquake in 747. When the Crusaders tried to capture it in the 11th Century, it had long been wrecked and given to sun and sand.

Before going in, I studied the relief map of the ruins under a glass case, which showed all the itineraries and landmarks. Fending off the volunteers to guide us, we headed for the south gate. It is one of four in a wall two miles long that once surrounded the city, and of which little remains.

Standing on a hill and dominating the Roman town a temple of Zeus. It was built in 2nd Century AD. At present only its stout walls remain, but further digging and repair will restore it to its original grandeur. It rises on two levels, linked by a flight of vaulted stairs. Above was the Temenos – the Sacred Enclosure – the place of sacrifice.

Next to the Temple of Zeus is one of the finest and best preserved Roman amphitheatres in the world. So remarkable are its acoustics that a whisper on the stage can be clearly heard across the auditorium to the remotest of the back seats. The stone backdrop of carved pilasters, niches and statues changes colour with the light from milky white to conch-shell pink, glittering yellow and burnished ochre. Now the amphitheatre is used for concerts and plays at the annual Jerash International Arts Festival in July.

'Stand on the little circle in the middle and sing, and see what happen,' Gibril suggested. As we were alone and had the place to ourselves, I did. The sound echoed round the circular space several times before receding like waves at sea, then died to a whisper.

I climbed the steep 32 levels to where spectators sit on a

vertiginous ridge for a sweeping view of the city: its oval forum surrounded by 56 Ionic columns; its mile-long street of 240 massive columns, which were hauled across the desert from Aswan in Egypt to support an aqueduct and bring fresh water to the whole city. From here one can also see the shrine of the Nymphs, goddesses of fertility who were thought to bathe here at night, and the Temple of Artemis, presiding goddess of Jerash. The temple's tall columns seem to join Heaven and Earth along the skyline. In subsequent times, several Byzantine churches were built out of its wreckage, and some of the floor mosaics showing local birds and plants have survived.

The street of columns leads on to two main crossroads. At each of these crossings four bases once supported tall statue-bearing columns. Today only the bases remain, and Gibril pointed out the scallop-shaped niches scooped into them for oil lamps to light the way at night. Further along we stopped by a nymphaeum, built in 191 AD, on two levels, with an elaborately carved marble and plaster facade. Water once cascaded from great urns held by its statues into a large pool, flowed away through carved lions' jaws and then along the street below. Today it is dry, but the marble facade shows pink and honey-coloured in the changing light.

'At night when the town goes to sleep, the nymphs need to come and play in the fountain,' Gibril told me. 'You know the word nymphomaniac?'

'Yes, but where did you learn it?' I asked.

'From tourists. You are the first one who hasn't mentioned it. They always say "nymphomaniac" and laugh when I tell them about nymphs swimming in the pool. How come you didn't say it?'

'I was thinking of something else, trying to imagine the way people lived in those days. Not all Westerners are sex-obsessed, Gibril.'

Further along we came at last to the Temple of Artemis. This was built in 2nd Century AD, and two flights of stairs lead from a massive porphylaeum – great gate – to a courtyard where the temple stands in a square surrounded by columns. The main shrine stood on a platform and was enclosed by 45 feet tall Corinthian columns. Only the double row in front still stand, but one can see that this temple to the Hunter Goddess, whom the Romans called Diana, was once the most awe-inspiring sacred edifice in the city.

Jerash is an example of the Roman genius for laying out towns. They achieved a perfect harmony of the sacred and the profane; the individual and the communal were blended in a single aesthetic whole. Among the ruins, my imagination heightened by solitude, heat and the dazzling midday, I could conjure up the bustling Roman city, its forum with toga-clad elders in session, its rows of shops behind the colonnades, its warren of alleys and women crowding around the fountain. I could almost hear the rumble and clatter of chariots along the main thoroughfares – their wheels have left deep grooves in the paving stones. Suddenly songs of exaltation of desert larks out of a clear blue sky brought me back to the present.

Across a small river, the flat-roofed huddle of houses and the narrow lanes of modern Jerash are an incongruous intrusion on the eternal silence of the ruins.

We sat in the shade of vine trellis at the nearby Guest House Restaurant amid roses, jasmines and oleanders in bloom and had a lunch of grilled lamb and aubergine. Gibril went to meet a friend, whom he brought back, and we talked over coffee.

Hasham too was a driver, but he spoke fluent English. He was in his late thirties – dark, stocky, well-groomed and exuding energy and warmth. Unlike Gibril, he had no inhibitions about strong opinions, mostly about politics. He was a born-again Muslim, he informed me. 'But I'm not fanatic,' he added reassuringly. 'I was naughty, very naughty – smoke, drink, women... Then I realise waste of time, and I change. Islam is clear – everything is in the Book, the Holy Koran. It was written by God and sent to the Prophet. It has everything you need for this life and the next. But people is stupid, not read book, invent things instead.'

Hasham had stopped working during the Gulf War to help the refugees – the Indian, Pakistani, Palestinian and Egyptian workers who had poured in their tens of thousands over the frontier into Jordan. He defended Saddam: 'He gave us our oil free,' he said. 'But he was stupid. He made three big mistakes: letting the Western hostages go, not attacking Saudi Arabia at the same time as Kuwait and taking over its oil installations and finally, having made these stupid mistakes, not accepting peace. Yes, he was very stupid!'

He put all his anger and frustration into 'stupid' – hissing the word out like a cornered snake. His *bêtes noires* were the oil-rich Emirates, Kuwait and, above all, Saudi Arabia: 'They chop off a poor man's hand for stealing a loaf of bread, but waste millions of Arab money on weapons, gambling and bad women...'

It occurred to me that the poor in Arab countries consider oil as a gift from God to Muslims, regardless of man-made frontiers, and that despite their alleged fatalism they harbour deep resentment at the discrepancy between the rich few and the deprived millions. The minuet of meetings and hugs and treaty-signing between their rulers leaves them cold. Their reactions cover a whole range of feelings between Hasham's passionate anger and Gibril's cynical resignation. What a fertile ground for demagogues to transform the young and innocent into killers!

I went to have a look at the bronze camels, Bedouin dolls and prayer beads on sale nearby. The stallholders did not press their wares, unusual in such places. Could it be that the proud, aristocratic dignity of the Bedouin has somehow survived in modern commercial Jordan?

'We will take the long road back to see more things,' Gibril announced; so instead of going straight back to Amman, he drove me on a long loop to the west. It is often small detours and unexpected events that make a journey interesting. We drove through beautiful pine woods and olive groves to Aljun, which is about twenty miles from Jerash. It is famous for its mediaeval castle, Qal'at-al-Rabad, which stands on a hill four thousand feet high, two miles from the modern town. It was built there in 1184 by Azzadin Ausama bin Munqidh, one of Saladin's generals, to stem the tide of the Crusaders' advance from Damascus and Jerusalem and to protect the caravans and pilgrims crossing the desert. It is a great example of Islamic military architecture and was one of a chain of fortresses whose beacons and pigeon-stages carried messages from Baghdad to Cairo in a day.

It is said that the castle was built on the site of an ancient monastery and that Aljune was the name of an old monk who lived there before its destruction – by earthquake, it is thought. So when Azzadin's men built the castle, they named it after its last Christian inhabitant. Today only a cross carved on one of the stone blocks of the walls alludes to its Christian origin.

The castle was destroyed by the Mongols in the 13th Century, rebuilt almost immediately and further fortified by the Mameluke Sultan Baibar. The 14th Century Maghrebin traveller Ibn Batuta visited Aljun in 1344 and described it as 'a fine town with good markets and a strong castle; a stream runs through the town and its waters are sweet and good'. Aljun's later history is obscure, but it was used briefly by the Ottomans in the 17th Century and finally abandoned. When the traveller J. L. Burkhardt discovered it in 1812, forty people still lived in its dark precincts. Later, what its successive conquerors had not destroyed, the earthquakes of 1837 and 1927 completed, and it remained lost until recently, when its possibilities as a site were discovered, and part of it was restored.

Here I accepted the help of Foad, sole guide and guardian of the castle. We were the only visitors, and he seemed to need them. He was a plump, slow-moving, middle-aged man, with a benevolent smile and a mother-of-pearl rosary, which he seemed to use as an *aide-mémoire*, looking at it thoughtfully before mentioning dates and names.

Up many perilous flights of stairs we climbed, through vaulted halls, private chambers, dark kitchens, windowless bathrooms, neglected stables and sentry posts. We wandered through the abandoned quarters of Saladin's army: 'There used to be a drawbridge here; horses crossed it and mounted the stone steps,' Foad explained as we entered. One could almost see the horses panting up the steps and hear the clatter of their hooves…

'They poured boiling oil over the enemy soldiers,' he said, pointing to the holes in the floor of the upper storeys; 'if their arrows didn't get them first,' he added, swivelling his eyes towards the window-slits. How many were slaughtered by such ingenious and gruesome methods before the fortress was captured or renounced, I wondered. How did they survive through long sieges, droughts, penury? And what of their lives in peace time?

The castle has four vast halls on various floors: one for storage, now dark and cavernous, another for horses and other stabling, a third for the soldiery and finally a long, handsomely vaulted assembly hall for the leaders. This has been turned into a refectory, and a large party of Germans were feasting on

Oriental dishes spread on a long array by the wall. The meal had ended, but the cook hospitably offered me a cup of cardamom-scented coffee and a delicious baklava.

Beside the halls were the living quarters. You can still see where the cooking took place by blackened walls. Foad explained how rainwater from the roof was collected and channelled into cisterns. From the roof a breathtaking view sweeps on all sides over green oases, wooded hills, rivers and, to the east, the desert that covers 80% of Jordan. I sat down on a flat stone to contemplate the landscape and savour the cool air. 'I'll tell you a story,' said Foad after a while, crouching on the ground beside me: 'There was once an American poet his name was Rowbert Froast [Robert Frost], and he wrote one poem called "Stopping By Woods On Snowy Evenings". In it he is riding his horse through snowy fields, and he stop to enjoy the view and forget about time. Suddenly his horse shake his harness bells and he wake up from his dream. So he say:

> "The woods are lovely, dark, and deep
> "But I have promises to keep
> "And miles to go before I sleep."

This poem has two meanings – write them down, lady! – first that he is enjoying the view but must think of other obligations, and second that we enjoy life but we are going back to God. So come along, lady, you have a long way to go too.'

'We have time to see the sunset by the Dead Sea – it is beautiful,' offered Gibril, by way of yet another extra-itinerary treat. We drove through the Jordan Valley, 'the fruit and vegetable basket of Jordan', amid vineyards and olive groves, and polythene greenhouses that covered the land like giant centipedes.

'Jordan's olive oil is the best in the world,' Gibril remarked.

'I've tasted all the others – Italian, Greek, Spanish – all less good. Here the rain waters the trees and they make good fruit.'

'What rain?' I asked. 'The country is dry ten months a year.'

'We have rain in winter. The trees are strong; they manage.'

To prove his point, he made a detour to an olive oil factory. It was a hangar containing a spiky red dinosaur that roared and snarled as it guzzled sackfuls of olives, crushed the fruit with its iron jaws, churned and squeezed the pulp and spewed out green nectar. Despite an overpowering smell, the place seemed a social focus, full of men hanging about, watching the writhing beast and talking to each other, while dozens of children milled around. They all wanted their photographs taken. A tiny, thin man, his face disfigured by scars, his teeth a line of black stumps, began to organise everybody. On his instructions they struck theatrical poses and composed groups, smiling to the camera as I clicked away. Then the man himself posed by the doorway, thrusting his chest forward and looking into the distance, like the tenor in a village opera performance. They asked me to taste the oil – very strong but delectable – and followed me to the car, as if I were a pied piper or some creature from outer space.

'Foreigners don't come here often, so they like to see you,' Gibril explained.

We reached Suweimeh on the Dead Sea as the sun sank behind the hills of the West Bank on the far shore, a fiery orb leaving a gold trail over the wavelets. A few bathers were floating in the water, so saline that it is impossible to sink; one was reading a book! Women swimming in their clothes looked like mermaids gambolling in a pool.

I sipped iced tea on the terrace of a beach café and contemplated the scene. Straining the eyes, one can just discern the minarets and belfries of Jerusalem in the distance, a floating chimera which vanishes as darkness falls. Presently, the sun disappeared below the horizon, leaving a warm afterglow. All around, the landscape stirred with nightfall activity: a line of camels ambled along the road on the edge of the desert; flocks of goat and sheep led by tiny shepherds jingled towards their shelters; starlings and blackbirds flew in formation in the indigo sky – an Abrahamic scene of timeless serenity.

We drove back to Amman in complete silence.

In August 1812, J. L. Burkhardt set out from Damascus to Cairo on a journey across the thousand-mile desert. As he reached Jordan, one of his Bedouin guides told him of an extraordinary ruined city hidden in a fastness of the mountains. It lay off his path, in Wadi Musa, or the Valley of Moses.

He made the detour but, to avoid suspicion, pretended that he wanted to sacrifice a goat at Aaron's tomb; this was on the summit of the highest mountain in the chain, which command-ed a view of the whole area. Deep in the valley he found some ancient tombs and obelisks; then he was led into a narrow and winding gorge more than a mile long, as if the rocks had been thrust asunder by lightening. It was called the Siq. He emerged into an astonishing assembly of ancient temples, theatres, banqueting halls and tombs, hewn, most of them, out of the red sandstone of the gorge. Some Bedouin families had pitched their tents among them. 'It appears very probable that the ruins in Wadi Musa are those of ancient Petra,' he wrote in his diary on 22nd August. Lost for eight centuries, the Atlantis of the desert had been revealed to the world once again.

Until the 1930s, only an adventurous handful of travellers had made the journey to Petra, and in the 1950s it still took ten days on horseback or a whole day in a jeep to reach it from Amman. Today the Desert Highway has cut the distance down to three hours, and 'The Eighth Wonder of the World', the 'Rose-Red City Half as Old as Time', can be seen in a day.

Gibril and I set out at dawn. By chance, my trip coincided with the country's first democratic general election. The autumn air was vibrant with excitement; towns and villages were festooned with bright banners and posters, as if for a festival. Throngs of people, some in traditional jelabas and red or black chequered head scarves – kaffieh – or blue jeans and t-shirts, gathered in village squares to listen to speeches, debate and argue about the candidates, whose photographs hung everywhere. My foreign appearance attracted attention, and young people surrounded me to try their out English, offer hospitality and ask questions.

Jordan used to be ruled in a tribal manner, with the king providing a focus of consensus and social cohesion, reigning as well as ruling, 'the loving father of his people'. With his genius for survival and alertness to changes – most notably the revolution of 1979 in Iran, the rise of Islamic fundamentalism and Saddam Hussein's growing and rapacious appetite for power – King Hussein started introducing democracy, with a partial general election in 1989. Eighty Deputies were elected to a House of Representatives; the 'Islamist' party gained 24 seats, and, integrated within the democratic process, could not complain if the reactionary measures they proposed were rejected by the parliamentary majority. Nor could they block the ratification of new and more progressive laws.

One novelty alone stuck in their gullets: among the eighty successful candidates, one woman Deputy had been elected. Toujan Faisal is a popular television presenter in her forties, married and with children. The Islamists charged her with apostasy (for which the penalty is death), dragged her in front of an 'Islamic' tribunal and dug up some item of Sharia law which forces a husband to divorce an apostate wife and take away her children. Hanan Hadravi, herself a university professor, told me the story: 'To his credit her husband remained staunchly loyal to her, and finally the opposition accepted defeat.' Emboldened by her success, other women stood this time for election; however, only Madam Faisal would win back her seat.

We drove along an old Roman road that hair-pinned through the scorched mountains. In the canyons, Bedouin tents huddled, and flocks of goats and sheep grazed. Madaba is a Byzantine city with remarkable mosaics, destroyed by an earthquake in 747 and rebuilt in the 19th Century. We halted to explore. Many of the ancient mosaics are now inside modern houses which were built over the ruins of the old city. The most outstanding of them is a pilgrim's map of the Holy Land on the floor of St George's Church. It depicts the area between the Mediterranean coast and Jerusalem in a variety of vivid primary colours on a white sandstone base. Though accurate in detail, it is clearly less of a geographical plan than a map of salvation, leading the pilgrim through Christ's journey from His baptism in the Jordan River to His tomb in the Church of Holy Sepulchre.

A friend of Gibril's offered us a cup of tea in his shop, and I bought a mother-of-pearl rosary for a friend; then we drove to Mount Nebo, six miles to the northwest of Madaba. From its summit, a view stretches over the Dead Sea to the Mount of Olives. It is where Moses is believed to have first cast his eyes on the Promised Land and to have spent the last years of his life. A simple monument marks the tomb which is thought to be his. In the 1930s, a group of Franciscan monks bought the site and began excavations. They discovered mosaic floors and walls, fragments of masonry and marble, now protected by a roof and walls. Still more remarkable are the mosaics in a 6th Century church in the biblical town of Nebo itself, two miles down the road, showing a Tree of Life and wild and tame animals. There was no guardian or official. I was told that Franciscan monks and nuns are still living there, down in the valley. I sat and gazed at the grand view, wondering whether the longing in the soul for a safe haven could ever be assuaged. Or is the real Promised Land always beyond the horizon? Did God spare Moses, his mission in this world accomplished, further travails and disappointments?

Fifty miles to the south along the Desert Highway, we arrived at the Karak des Chevaliers, the grandest of a chain of castles, strategically spaced out by a day's march between each, which the Crusaders built on mountaintops From Byzantium to the Gulf of Aqaba on the Red Sea. The Knights cultivated the surrounding valleys and levied tolls from caravans, and at night their fire signals went from castle to castle, until they reached Jerusalem. The Karak's history is replete with tales of chivalry, intrigue, drama and romance. Its massive walls and battle-ments, now secured against further deterioration, surround double-vaulted galleries, rooms, stables and sentry posts and give a convincing idea of the vast population it once harboured. The castle resisted Muslim attack and siege for 50 years, but fell to Saladin in 1189.

We finally reached Petra at dusk. 'We have time to see the Spring of Moses before night falls,' said Gibril, guiding me to a pool full of cold clear water. Moses is believed to have struck the rock here and released a spring which has been flowing ever since.

A thriving little town has grown up on the hills around Petra, with hotels and shops. I stayed in the Anbat Hotel, the first, no-star hotel built in Petra. The staff, of young and well-educated Bedouins, made up with kindness and good manners for any absence of luxury.

At dawn the next morning, pandemonium raged in the valley. Bedouins and tourists were haggling over horses for a ride through the Siq. 'I'm the best guide in the world!' said Yusof, a lean and wiry young Bedouin who worked in my hotel. 'My cousin study archaeology, and he teach me everything he learn from his teachers.' Yusof chain-smoked and drove a hard bargain, but he turned out to be a wonderful companion: he sang beautiful love songs, quoted reams of poetry and, aged 25, lamented his vanished youth.

Inside the Siq, a narrow path runs between rocks rising sheer to four hundred feet, the sky a blue thread above. Plants and trees sprout from cracks wherever there is roothold. I emerged in front of the Khaznat – or Treasury – a stunningly beautiful rose-red two-storey tomb caved out of the rock-face, glowing in the sun as if light is actually being diffused from it through a diaphanous veil. In legends, brigands used to bury hoards of gold and jewellery inside it, hence its name. More recently, it has been the scene of the final contest between Good and Evil in Stephen Spielberg's *Indiana Jones*.

The origins of Petra are lost, but centuries before our era some nomadic Nabataeans settled in the valley, levied tolls from caravans passing between Arabia and Syria and made it the capital of a rich trading state. The Romans captured it in 106 AD and turned it into a Roman city. They were followed by the Byzantines and then the Muslims, but Petra declined into oblivion when the maritime route through the Red Sea replaced the overland trail and was eventually forgotten.

Beyond the Khaznat, the cliff-face on either side is a phantasmagoria of tombs and temples and dwellings. Inside them the striated rocks of the walls form mesmerising rainbows of iridescent blue, green and pink. Fragments of the ancient clay conduits that fed the city with water are still there, high up on the mountainside.

Further along, I reached the remains of the 2nd Century Roman city, with its amphitheatre, temples, triumphal arches and colonnaded main street.

'The Magi must have come through Petra,' said Yusof. 'Maybe Jesus himself stopped here'.

We rested in the shade of one of the acacia trees that have sprouted among the ruins and watched little boys making intricate pictures with coloured sand inside bottles. Bedouin women offered decorated donkeys for the climb to the monastery on the summit: 'Good price! For you good price!' they pressed. I decided to walk – a hard fifty minute climb, up the narrow, rocky path.

The largest Nabataean edifice, the monastery is the tomb of a 3rd Century king, turned into a church by the Byzantines. From its ridge, a magnificent view unfolds – rows of flame-coloured mountains and Wadi Arba beyond, stretching from the Dead Sea to the Red Sea.

Back at the centre, there was lunch at tables set up in the shade of lime trees; you take this before attempting the climb to the High Place of Sacrifice – a two-hour trek along a tortuous path among vertiginous rocks. The summit has been flattened to make a wide platform for the priest and the congregation, while runnels show where blood flowed out:

'They anoint the goat in the temple below and bring it up here to kill,' Yusof explained.

The next morning we left Petra at daybreak and drove south to Wadi Rum. (Inevitably, one is told that David Lean's film *Lawrence of Arabia* was shot here.) Gigantic red rocks rise sheer a thousand feet from the ground, while behind them rows of white sandstone mountains stretch to infinity like clouds – monuments to eternity sculpted by time. You can hire a camel or a jeep or walk through the Wadi. I chose the jeep, and we bumped our way for miles among the jagged rocks without encountering a soul. A hawk flew out from a rock-face, followed its shadow on the sand and soared away in the limpid blue. Inside the clefts of the mountains, we found rainwater pools and Nabataean inscriptions. A little shepherd was splashing water over his head and face while his goats clambered on the rocks in search of tufts of thorn, their bells jingling. He cupped his hands full of water and offered it to me. I bent down and drank it – never was a drink more welcome, nor more winningly offered.

In the past, the Wadi was dotted with black Bedouin tents and alive with activity. Now all but a fraction of the nomads have been settled in villages. 'Modern women don't want to spend their lives gathering twigs for firewood and walking miles to fill their pitchers,' said Gibril.

So that the visitors can catch a glimpse of Bedouin life, one tent has been turned into a teahouse, with carpets and cushions and a charcoal brazier. We sipped a glass of sweet tea and listened to an old, emaciated musician playing a one-string fiddle and singing a haunting lovesong. 'In the old days you got it free. Now you have to pay and tip the singer!' Gibril said to me apologetically.

On our way back to Amman, we drove sixty miles east of the city to Azraq (well-known as Azrak from T. E. Lawrence's *The Seven Pillars of Wisdom*), the only oasis in the eastern desert. In the past, thousands of birds migrating from Europe lived in its spring-water pools and marshes during the winter – some two hundred species were counted by Julian Huxley in 1948 – and many animals, including ibexes, roamed its grasslands. Precious little wildlife can be found here today: 'What animals?' said Gibril. 'In Jordan we only have people, too much people.' The marshes have been drained and their waters diverted to Amman. With a high birthrate, like many parts of the Third World, Jordan is torn between development and conservation. Azraq has now been declared a National Park, but will the birds remember their lost paradise and come back? Can the extinct fauna be reintroduced?

Meanwhile, I saw little sign here of the 'luminous, silky Eden' that Lawrence described. He chose its 13th Century castle as his headquarters during his campaign against the Turks in 1917. The castle is a ruin now, but the great gate and his upstairs room have been restored in his memory.

'Next time you come to Jordan you must go to Aqaba,' Gibril suggested as we left. The Red Sea town on the southern tip of Jordan, only fifty miles from Petra, with its translucent seas and coral reefs and amazing fishes has become a favourite haunt of divers.

'I promise to come back,' I said, and I meant it.

As we drove towards Amman, the sky suddenly darkened. The horizon became a thick black curtain, and the wind rose, sweeping sand over the road in sheets. All traffic halted, and cars piled up for miles, while dust penetrated our car and filled our eyes, nostrils and mouths. For a moment, I thought that everything – the highway, the vehicles and the people – would be buried under mountains of shifting sand, to be rediscovered centuries later. 'THE END' seemed to appear on a cosmic screen. Amazingly, nobody panicked, and, after an hour or so, thunder resounded through the desert, lightening ripped the black clouds on the horizon, heavy rain began to fall and the cars gradually began to move.

SYRIA

To the Gates of Eden

*This is the Paradise which the righteous have
been promised: It is watered by running streams:
eternal are its fruits, and eternal are its shades.
There shall flow in it rivers of unpolluted waters.*

– The Holy Koran

*Nay, stand thou back; I will not budge a foot:
This be Damascus, be thou cursed Cain,
To slay thy brother Abel, if thou wilt.*

– Shakespeare, *Henry VI, Part 2*

'A city with trees and rivers and fruits and birds, as though
it were a paradise.' So is Damascus described in
A Thousand and One Nights. It boasts of being the oldest city in
the world, older than history. Some say that it was founded by
Damashq, the slave of Abraham, presented to him by Nimrod.
The historian Josephus attributes its foundation to Uz, great-
grandson of Noah and son of Aram, whose descendants are the
Arameans. Archaeologists have found remnants of chalcolithic
people who lived by its rivers in the fifth millennium before
Christ. The Damascenes believe that it is even older, that here

was the original Garden of Eden, where God fashioned Adam from the mud of the river Barada – Abana in the Bible. They say that Christ Himself came here once and Muhammad twice, and we know how the blinded St Paul walked along The Street Called Straight to the house of Ananias and was healed.

Today the road to Damascus is in the sky, and it ends at the city's international airport. For years Syria was a secret country, considered a backer of terrorism and stooge of the Soviet Union. This unfavourable image, together with the civil war in Lebanon and the unsettled state of the region, discouraged the traveller. Those adventurers who visited the country came back enchanted by its antiquities and its people, but told tales of economic stagnation and political oppression.

Since the collapse of Communism and the end of the civil war in Lebanon, Syria has opened up to the West and, as if to make up for lost time, welcomes foreign visitors. But the rusty machinery of a centralised economy is not easy to dismantle, and, as in Eastern Europe, there is little infrastructure to service a full-blown Western-style market economy. Yet there is evidence of change – luxury hotels and apartment blocks in new residential areas, Mercedeses and BMWs galore and the extensive restoration of historical sites all attest to a measure of liberalisation and prosperity.

I longed to visit Syria for years. When I was a child, my mother made the pilgrimage to Mecca and returned laden with presents: lengths of printed crêpe-de-Chine, gold bracelets and silk stockings, all from the bazaar in Damascus. The city has always been an obligatory stop on the pilgrims' route; my mother described its rivers and gardens, monuments and shrines, and my imagination was fired. Decades passed, but the image endured, helped by homesickness. Recently I met Iffat, a Syrian scholar of English literature who was translating one of my books, and she asked me to call on her in Damascus. This reignited my long-held desire, and off I eventually went.

The best panorama of Damascus is from Mount Qassioun to the north, part of the Anti-Lebanon range. Its foothills are now prosperous suburbs, with modern villas, restaurants and cafés, but a few miles further up the villages are full of legends: Abraham was born here, in the village of Burzah; and when Cain slew Abel, he was punished by having to carry his corpse on his shoulders and roam these hills for forty years. In the end he buried his dead brother in a cave, but 'his blood reaches from about halfway up the mountain, and God has preserved red traces of it on the stones', wrote Ibn Jubayr, a 12th Century traveller, who visited 'the cave of blood' in 1184. The rocks have mostly crumbled away, but red patches still show on the mountainside.

At dusk, the view stretches over a vast fairground, twinkling with millions of multi-coloured lights, above which rise dozens of slender minarets, like a Heaven-bound fleet of rockets. Beyond, to the east, the green canopy of Ghouta, a district famous for its orchards, fades into the limitless desert. They say that when the Prophet Muhammad first gazed upon Ghouta in full blossom, he covered his eyes: it seemed wrong to see Paradise before he went there.

In daytime, the same view reveals a dense jungle of drab concrete, covered with a quivering pall of pollution. The river Barada, which gave birth to the city, is now a shallow stream choked with rubbish, its green banks swallowed by urban sprawl. Syria has one of the world's highest birthrates, and within a generation the population of Damascus has trebled; it is now three million. To house it, hideous grey cubicles, reminiscent of Eastern Europe, have been built by the government. For more than thirty years, the country has been ruled by the Baath Socialist party, with President Hafez Assad at its head.

His Big Brother presence is everywhere – photos, busts and statues of all sizes never out of sight. Stability is the result – no Islamic fundamentalism, no terrorism, no sectarian wars between ethnic and religious minorities, no beggars; but also no dissent. 'We do not speak about politics,' everyone tells you, from bazaar merchants and artisans to office employees and taxi-drivers. 'To be fair, the Assad régime is paternalistic, benevolent by the standards of the region,' says an English journalist, expert on the Middle East. 'As long as you don't try to topple the government, you can criticise individual politicians, the bureaucracy, the corruption endemic in Third World countries. It is not like Iraq, where the slightest dissent is punished by torture and death, or Saudi Arabia where women are virtually locked up.' He believes that market forces and tourism will in time loosen things further.

If modern Damascus is like any other Third World town – a vast building site where it is hard to distinguish between what is being put up and what pulled down – Old Damascus lives up to romantic expectations: a bustling Levantine metropolis strewn with the shreds of its long history. Strolling along the crowded streets is like being at a feast: shops and pavements overflow with fruit and vegetables – mounds of watermelons, pomegranates, figs, grapes, aubergines and courgettes – all for a fraction of their price in Europe. A parade of regional and tribal costumes unfolds, while street pedlars sell you sherbet, rose-water ices, corn-on-the-cob, walnuts and pistachios. A scent of jasmine floats in the air.

I try to go by bus or taxi when I am in a new country, as it brings me into contact with local people. In Damascus, taxis are plentiful and fairly cheap, and once in the Old City one can walk everywhere. But my time was limited, so I rented a car with a driver.

My driver was Abdel-Qader. Qader means mighty, and it is

one of the 99 attributes of God. Abdel-Qader is 'The Slave of the Almighty'. I called him just Almighty, which was fitting, as he had a solution for every problem, knew everyone of interest and was full of humour. Our only disagreement was over his refusal to let me pay for anything. Syrian hospitality is legendary, even by the high standards of the Middle East – I was a guest, and a *woman*, and his honour would be at risk. Yet he had a large brood to feed – ten children, and, at forty, with a 36 year old wife, more could be coming along.

Ten? Aghast, I mumbled something about birth control. Almighty had not thought of it. No wonder the country's population is exploding. As soon as he learnt I was of Persian origin – 'one of us' – he took to walking a few steps ahead, like a pasha, and upbraided me for not eating enough and being 'always in the books' and ruining my eyes. In the following days, we explored as much of the country as we could, and with Almighty's broken English and my few words of Arabic we got on perfectly. 'Language not matter,' he declared at the outset. I agreed.

At the crossroads of East and West, bordered by the Euphrates on one side and the Mediterranean on the other, Syria was coveted and conquered by successive imperial powers – Babylonian, Greek, Roman, Persian and Byzantine – before Islam swept through the region in the 7th Century. Syria is strewn with their vestiges, and all of them have left their marks on Damascus. You can find Greek, Roman and Arabic inscriptions at different levels on the same wall. The Roman wall round the city is five miles long, with eight gates – Bâb in Arabic – 'The Gates of Paradise'. When in 395 the Roman empire was divided in two, Syria became part of the Eastern half, Byzantium, and Damascus remained an important trading centre. In the 6th Century, the Sassanian Persians defeated the Byzantines and imposed their dominion over the region. But wars had so exhausted the two empires that neither could resist the onslaught of the new power arising in the Arabian desert. In August 636, only four years after the death of the Prophet, the Muslim armies defeated the Byzantines at the famous battle of Yarmouk and conquered Syria, ending over a thousand years of European rule. But Muslim Syria was not safe from predators either: the Crusaders, the Mongols and Tamerlane succeeded each other, until in 1561 the Ottoman Sultan Selim took Damascus and annexed the whole region. Thereafter, for five hundred years, Syria was a province of the Ottoman Empire and ruled by a pasha. In the aftermath of the World War I, the victorious Allies dismantled that empire and divided the Middle East between England and France, giving the latter mandates over Lebanon and Syria. After several nationalist uprisings were crushed by the French, the country finally achieved independence in 1948, and Damascus became the capital of the newly created republic of Syria. The influence of France endured through the French language, but English has gradually supplanted it.

Damascus is packed with mosques and madrassahs, or theological colleges, Byzantine churches, Turkish bazaars and hammams and khans (public baths and caravanserais). Towering above them is an 11th Century citadel (Qasr). The Umayyads conquered Syria in 661 and made Damascus the seat of the caliphate and capital of the first Arab dynasty. Their spirit still haunts the city, with the Great Umayyad Mosque at its centre, the fourth holiest in the Islamic world after Mecca, Medina and the Dome of the Rock. The mosque began as a temple of Jupiter, became a Byzantine cathedral and was converted to its present use in 715.

At the entrance, I was given an abaya to cover my head, took off my shoes and entered a vast courtyard paved with marble and mosaic, surrounded by two-storey arcades, with a fountain in the centre where men were making their ablutions. They say that the fountain marks the mid-point between Mecca and Constantinople and that caravans of pilgrims from all over the world bound for the House of God in Mecca converged here to pray before crossing the Arabian desert. Peace and harmony pervade the atmosphere, as if centuries of faith and piety have drawn an invisible curtain between time and eternity. Even a flock of birds crossing the limpid sky were hushed, only their shadows on the marble flagstones marking their passage. Here and there men prayed in solitude, bending and prostrating themselves, oblivious to the world. A large Byzantine mosaic on the courtyard wall depicts an arcadian scene of trees and villas which match the early travellers' descriptions of Ghouta, its gardens and orchards, to the east.

Inside the grand prayer chamber, a hundred lanterns light up a forest of columns, while men and women pray on the carpeted floor. On one side is a simple shrine to St John the Baptist, whose head was apparently sent here to the Roman Emperor by Herod. Presently, the silence is broken by the muezzin's chant from the Minaret of Jesus, so called because, according to a legend, Jesus Christ will come down through it on the Day of Judgement. A second minaret, of the Bride, is named after a caliph's wife, whose rich father roofed the great building with lead.

In contrast to the emptiness and silence in the nave (as it were) of the mosque, the Shrine of Hossein, in a room off the east arcade, was full of garrulous pilgrims, most of them from Iran. The air was vibrant with exaltation. Hossein, grandson of the Prophet and third of the twelve Imams of Shiism, contested the legitimacy of the Umayyads' caliphate, raised an army to fight them and was killed at the battle of Karbala (in present-day Iraq) in 680. His severed head was brought to Caliph Yazid in Damascus and is kept in a casket surrounded by a grille. Murmuring prayers, the pilgrims jostled to touch and kiss the metal.

Round the corner from the Great Mosque is Saladin's tomb. Built in 1196, it is a tiny domed chamber in a charming little garden of scented creepers and fruit-laden citrus trees. It is a modest resting place for so great a hero, who was loved and praised by allies and adversaries alike and whose courage in battle matched his magnanimity in victory. Even Dante, who condemned the Prophet ('the Sower of Discord') to the 8th Circle of the Inferno, spared Saladin and confined him only to limbo.

Saladin defeated the Crusaders and recaptured Jerusalem in 1187; then he stormed their castles along the coast and seized the whole region from Euphrates to the Nile. When the French Commander, Général Gouraud, entered Damascus in 1920 to take up the French mandate, he went straight to Saladin's tomb and declared, 'Nous revenons, Saladin!' I wonder if he heard the hero's ghost whispering, 'Pas pour longtemps, mon ami!' More appropriate is the carving on his sarcophagus: 'Oh God, receive his soul and open to him the gates of Paradise, the last conquest for which he hoped.'

Emerging from the southern gate of the Great Mosque, I found myself in front of a Roman triumphal arch, gateway to the Temple of Jupiter, rising sixty feet above the surrounding buildings; I then plunged into the Souk Hamidiyeh, the main artery of the bazaar – a covered maze of shopping lanes, seething with local pilgrims, tourists, porters and hucksters. A medley of Druze and Bedouin costumes, the sing-song of hawkers, the tinkling of donkey and bicycle bells make the bazaar a perpetual carnival. I followed my nose through the labyrinth of souks with their scents and spices, din of metalworkers and dazzle of gold and jewellery. Shopkeepers offered me tea and coffee, which they do whether one wants to buy or not. At the meat souk, the fumes of roasting kebabs drew us to the stalls of shwarma – delicious layers of chicken, tomatoes and green peppers grilled and wrapped in bread-flaps.

Qader took me to Bakdash, a cavernous and crowded ice-cream parlour where two young men were churning huge vats of ambrosial ingredients and pounding it rhythmically with gigantic pestles in a sort of athletic drill. 'This is real, not made in machine,' Qader commented as we watched the attendants ladling the finished delicacy into bowls and sprinkling it with crimson arabesques of cherry syrup and crushed pistachios. The scent of rosewater and sweetness and swirl of the snowy cream in the blue transparent bowls brought back to me childhood memories of Persia.

We followed along bustling lanes. Here and there a studded door beneath a carved stalactite alcove opened onto the great courtyard of a khan. There are dozens of them in and around the bazaar, often turned into warehouses and workshops, their marble courtyards and wrought-iron balconies recalling times when merchants from East and West used to gather here to chatter and swap merchandise. The most impressive of them is the domed 18th Century Khan Assad Pasha, in the spice-and-seed market called Souk Buzurieh. It was in use until the beginning of the 20th Century, when the roof fell in. Its main dome, surrounded by eight smaller ones, has been set right again, and the swirling patterns of black-and-white stone on the walls and the pendatives – ablaq – are a Syrian decorative invention. From the top we could see the roofscape of the bazaar, like an undulating Chinese paper dragon.

Further along, we came to the 12th Century Hammam Nurredin, the oldest in the city. It is named after Saladin's predecessor, who fought against the Crusaders and, by gaining control of Damascus, prepared the way for Saladin's final victory. He is buried in the nearby Madrassah Nourriyeh. I remembered the hammams of my childhood and longed to go in, but it was 'men only' day. The attendant allowed me to peep inside: a fountain full of gold fish and rose-petals murmured in the middle of a patio surrounded by carpet-covered ledges for reclining upon. A man in loincloth, leaning on a cushion, was smoking a nargileh; steam emanated from the hot chambers beyond. 'For one dollar you get full massage and scrub and coffee,' said Qader, whose salary allowed such indulgences only rarely.

The valiant Nurredin gave his name to Damascus's first free hospital, Bimarestan, and medical school as well. It was built in 1154, and the best surgeons and physicians of the Middle Ages trained and worked here, Muslim and Jewish. Islam rejects the notion of pain as punishment for Original Sin, and Muslim doctors invented anaesthetics with alcohol and belladonna. They plied their skills in the royal courts of Europe, and when their treatises were translated into Latin, their discoveries of medicinal plants and drugs and use of surgery contributed to the advance of medicine in the West. Today Bimarestan is a museum set around a tranquil shaded garden, where the only sound is the whisper of water in the fountain. The surrounding rooms exhibit the ancient world's surgical instruments, delicate glass containers and distilling apparatuses, frightening dental tools and stuffed animals. 'You see the talons of the hawk?' Qader pointed at a stuffed bird. 'They very strong! He catch a lamb and fifty men can't make him drop it – he prefer to die.' He told me that once a hawk's talon was caught in a trap, and the bird tore himself off to escape, leaving his foot behind.

In the library we saw illuminated manuscripts, drawings of the human nervous system by Elias Shirazi, a Persian Jew, and busts of Avicenna and other pioneers of medicine.

'You must have coffee!' decreed Almighty and took me down a flight of steps to Nawfarah – the Fountain – where men sat in groups under a vine trellis with their little cups, smoking nargileh. In the barber's shop at the side, a man was having a shave, another a haircut. I had heard of a shop selling pearls at half their London price. Qader knew where it was and led me there: a small first floor room, filled with cases of pearls. A few clients were examining and bargaining over strings of pearls from the Persian Gulf, the most lustrous and precious. 'Tourists are stupid!' said Qader as we left, jabbing his forehead and narrowing his eyes in indignation. 'They read in book and go there! I have one friend, very good man, I like. He is better for you.' A few yards further on, we found a minute shop where the same pearls cost half the price of ones in the other place. Despite my Middle Eastern background, I am no good at haggling and was lucky to have Qader do it for me. He invariably had 'one good friend' who gave him 'best price'.

Old Damascus is dotted with beautiful houses in decay. Some are beyond rescue, their upper floors almost touching across the narrow lanes. But now the government helps with renovations with grants and tax relief, and some have been redeemed. A successful example is The Umayyad's Palace, in the dyers' souk. Despite its name, this is a 19th Century seigneurial house, discriminatingly restored and made into one of Damascus's best restaurants. I went there that evening with my friend Iffat.

A series of patios is divided by arches, with carved ceilings and an oblong fountain; the floors and walls are covered with carpets and textiles and lit by lanterns of coloured glass. On one side as we went in, musicians sat on a carpet-covered dais, playing traditional Arab music, while a young velvety-voiced singer sang Sufi poems. Presently a whirling dervish appeared and began to dance. At first I was shocked by the idea – surely such spiritual rituals are not for show? But as the dervish's first tentative steps became a rapid gyration, his robes filling out in a circle and hands stretching between Heaven and Earth in a unifying axis, I was touched by the grace of it. 'Why not?' said Iffat, who is a practising Sufi. 'Anything that awakens consciousness and lifts the soul to a higher plane is good wherever it takes place.'

Afterwards, she took me to a Sufi zawyeh, or retreat, named after Abul-Shamat, a 19th Century sheikh (master) who was tutor to the last Ottoman sultan. This was in the populous Qanavat – Aqueduct – district, with derelict 18th and 19th Century wooden houses, where the Roman aqueduct used to supply the town with water. A vaulted entrance led to a garden where giant trees surrounded a pool. The present sheikh was not at home, but his family received us kindly, though it was late: 'Do you want to stay the night?' asked the young girl who showed us round. The place had the tranquillity and bareness of a monastery; the large prayer room was empty save for carpets and cushions on the floor and the founder's tomb in a recess. Here they hold sessions of prayers and Sufi chants on the eve of the Sabbath, which is on Friday. 'From the moment of creation to the Day of Judgement, time belongs to the dervish,' wrote a 14th Century Persian mystic. I, in the 20th Century, was bound by time: it was past midnight, and reluctantly we took our leave, but I wished I could have stayed longer in that timeless place.

Later a friend told me that, far from being saved, these magnificent houses are stripped of their panellings and decorations, which are then sold at auction houses in Europe and

America, with the connivance of Syrian officials. This is of course not an unusual tale in the Third World, where official government policies are one thing and what some of their corrupt members practice another. Yet these buildings are unique examples of an authentic architecture that combined beauty and comfort and suited the climate and culture of the country; they are part of a country's patrimony which, once lost, can never be recovered. 'People buy them for a fortune at the great auction houses in London and take them to Texas or South of France,' an English journalist told me.

In the morning Qader arrived early, and we set off for Takkiyeh Soleimanieh. It was built in 1554 by Sinan, the greatest Turkish architect, best known for his masterpieces in Istanbul and named after his patron Soleiman the Magnificent, who reigned until 1566. The mosque is on the south side of a garden with a pool and tall trees. Two graceful minarets rise either side of its ample dome. Columns of grey and pink marble, stained glass windows and fine tiles adorn the interior. All around the garden are arcaded buildings which were the quarters of whirling dervishes and later became a caravanserai for pilgrims. Now they have been converted to handicraft shops, while the refectory and kitchen have become a small military museum.

Next door, in the National Museum, has been assembled an impressive collection, ranging from the first alphabet, carved on a tiny cylinder three thousand years ago in Ugarit near the north coast, to a complete 19th Century Damascus drawing-room. The showpiece is the 2nd Century synagogue, brought from Doura Europas on the Euphrates and reconstructed here. The walls are covered with Biblical scenes: the crowning of King Solomon, the flight of the Jews from Egypt, and, although Judaism, like Islam, prohibits graven images and human likenesses, pictures of Abraham and the Prophets.

While I was visiting the museum, Almighty was drinking coffee with friends at the open-air café in the garden. I joined them: 'Only two days in Damascus?' they said, '*Wallah!*' (It is an exclamation of wonder.) 'You need two months at least.' Quite true. But I had already added a third day to my schedule: 'Europeans are always in a hurry! They waste life running. For what?' Almighty shook his head in pity.

We hurried to the Azam Palace, a magnificent mansion built by Assad Pasha, the powerful Ottoman governor of Damascus, in 1750. He employed the best artisans in the city, brought Roman columns from Bosra and ancient paving stones from Banias, and diverted water from Barada for his garden. When it was finished, the Palace had separate quarters arranged around courtyards: haremlek, the private apartments; selamlek, for offices and public functions. The Damascenes liked him, but he fell foul of the Sultan in the end; he was lured to Turkey, and strangled in a hammam. Today the Palace is a museum, where life-sized wax mannequins in original costume convey an impression of the pasha's daily life.

On our way back to the hotel, we stopped at the Roman citadel, which was enlarged by the Ayyubids – Saladin's dynasty – against the Crusaders. It was almost destroyed by the Mongols in 1260 and again by Tamerlane in 1400, then abandoned. The Ottomans used it as a jail and allowed it to decay. Recently repaired, it was teeming with tourists. We wandered through the cavernous vaulted halls that were once 'like a little town, having its own streets and houses', according to an 18th Century English traveller, and clambered over the roof where a grand view stretched over the city, bathed in the mellow light of the setting sun, the call of muezzins rippling through the air from every direction.

I remembered my mother extolling the mausoleum of Saida

Zeinab, one of the Prophet's granddaughters, in the southern outskirt of Damascus. Zeinab and her family were brought here as prisoners after her brother Hossein was defeated and killed by Yazid, the Umayyad caliph. Her eloquent and impassioned speech at Yazid's victory banquet is found in anthologies of Arabic prose as an example of the art of oratory. The mausoleum's high golden dome and tile-covered minarets loom on the horizon like chimeras in the desert. It is an important Shia shrine, and, in contrast to the severe Sunni mosques, the inside is palatial, with dozens of crystal chandeliers and Persian carpets and a dazzling gold and silver grill around the saint's tomb. The air quivers with exaltation; worshippers crowd round, clutching the metal work, whispering supplications and vows. 'One thousand pounds of gold has been used to cover the dome,' Qader informed me, given by the Saida's votaries from all over the world. 'You make a vow that if the saint makes you rich you will come back and pray at her tomb, and she will, that is sure.' I did not have the heart to ask why she had been remiss with *him*.

Back in town, we walked along The Street Called Straight, which leads to the Roman arch at the East Gate and the Christian area. Antique shops overflowed with icons, tiles, Bohemian glass, inlaid wood and brass artefacts, the fake and genuine casually mixed. 'How can I know this Greek icon is authentic?' I asked a dealer. 'You can't,' he admitted honestly. 'I take a risk; so do you.'

The house of Ananias is at the end of a picturesque side street. It is tiny, with enough room for only a dozen visitors at a time. The underground chapel was once the cellar of a 1st Century BC house, so at least the date fits St Paul's visit. A set of paintings on the walls of the adjoining room tell the story of his journey. A group of Italian nuns and their priest/guide were quietly praying before a simple altar. I stood at the back in order not to disturb them and pondered the story of this most crucial of Christian conversions.

Ananias must have been a common name in Damascus. Three men of that name are mentioned in *Acts of the Apostles*. The first is 'Ananias the liar', who with his wife Sapphira, cheated St Peter over a piece of property; both fell down dead when their deception was revealed (*Acts*, v). Another Ananias was the Jewish high priest who was an enemy of St Paul: when Paul was arrested for his preaching, he commanded the crowd to 'smite him on the mouth' (*Acts*, xxiii). The third was the man who is thought to have lived in this house: he was a fervent Christian who saw a vision of Jesus and carried His message to the temporarily blind Saul of Tarsus, whereupon 'there fell from his eyes as it had been scales: and he received sight forthwith, and arose, and was baptised' (*Acts*, ix). It occurred to me that Saul's journey is repeated in every soul, only the 'road to Damascus' varies for each.

We stopped for an early lunch at Casa Blanca, in the same street: a renovated, two-storey Ottoman family house, built around a patio covered with a glass dome, with wrought-iron balconies. It was like a greenhouse, with plants and flowers everywhere. Sadeq Fahri, the owner, ran a restaurant in Lyons for ten years but then fell homesick and came back: 'This was a ruin, but I knew I could rescue it.' We talked about exile and how homesickness grows with age, as the contours of memory blur and one forgets the reasons for having left, remembering only the good things – the love of family and friends.

Syrian Christians belong to several denominations, and each has churches in this area – Armenian, Syrian Catholic, Orthodox. We walked to the Greek Orthodox Patriarchal Church of the Virgin Mary but found it closed. It was getting late; I looked at my notes and realised how many important sites I had missed – churches, mosques, madrassahs, mausoleums...

'You see them next time,' said Qader.

We headed for the mountains.

The Anti-Lebanon range stretches along the length of Syria's coastline – a recumbent giant keeping watch between desert and sea. Its eastern flanks harbour many towns and villages of great historical interest within an hour's drive from Damascus. Two in particular are underlined on every travellers' itinerary.

Driving north along the Damascus-Homs highway, we took a secondary road towards Seidnaya to see the Convent of Notre Dame, famous for its miraculous icon of the Virgin Mary, believed to have been painted by St Luke the Evangelist. Called Our Lady of Seidnaya by the Crusaders, who made it a place of pilgrimage second only to Jerusalem, the convent stands on a platform jutting out from the mountainside, its pale silvery dome and clocktower rising above many-levelled cloisters and jasmine-clad courtyards. They say it was built where Noah planted the first vine. Byzantine sources believe it was founded by the Roman Emperor Justinian in 547. Legend has it that one day during the Persian wars Justinian was searching for a spring for his thirsty legions and, seeing a gazelle on the mountainside, pursued it to the summit of the rocks. As he drew his bow, he was dazzled by a flood of light – his quarry had turned into a beautiful woman dressed in white. 'You shall not kill me,' she said, 'but build for me a convent upon this rock.' And so he did, installing his own sister as its first Mother Superior. Today a lively little town has grown in the valley, catering for the thousands of pilgrims who visit every year.

As we climbed the steps to the entrance, Qader pointed to a marble slab, imprinted with a faint image of the Virgin: 'Women come here without babies, rub their hands on this and then on their tummies, and they have babies,' he explained. A protective grille around it was festooned with dakhils – strips of rag tied to the bars by worshippers while making a wish, in this case to become pregnant, with the promise to return if the wish is fulfilled. And indeed there was an unusual number of small children among the crowds of visitors – perhaps all gifts of the Blessed Virgin. 'But She performs other miracles, for Muslims too, heals the blind and the cripple,' a young nun told me later.

I made my way to the convent, walked in the shaded court-yards and climbed the stairs to catch a glimpse of the nuns' living quarters – a dormitory with tidy rows of iron beds, a kitchen where garrulous novices were preparing a meal and balconies garlanded with flowering creepers. The order belongs to the Greek Orthodox Church; the nuns' flowing black habits and head scarves cover them from tip to toe, leaving only their faces exposed – pale moons glimmering in a dark sky. They had ready smiles and seemed content. A young nun asked me where I came from. 'England,' I said. Most visi-tors are Christian Lebanese, followed by French and Italians. I asked her why she had chosen to become a nun? It was 'always the same questions!' she giggled; but to her the answer was simple – she had fallen in love with Christ and married Him. It was a safe bet, without fear of rejection or disappointment. Who would not envy the security of her eternally requited love?

I took my shoes off to enter the Chapel of the Virgin, a small dark room, its blue dome dotted with silver stars that twinkled in the light of myriad candles. A heady smell of incense and Oriental scents pervaded the air, hung in misty clouds from the draperies, rolled around the edges. The walls were encrusted with icons, some over a thousand years old, their images almost lost beneath centuries of grime and grease. Votive Fatimah's hands, filigreed charms, bits of gaudy jewellery and diamanté ornaments of no material value were pinned to the black cloth around the altar – tokens of faith and desire. Behind the altar a pair of small brass doors opened onto a recess where inside a silver casket is St Luke's picture of the Virgin. Legend goes that during the Middle Ages the Virgin wept and the Knights Templar collected her tears in phials and sent them back to Europe, believing them to be sovereign against blindness, sterility and storms at sea. Centuries of kisses and stroking have blurred the pigments, and a photographic facsimile is often used: a beautiful young woman regally dressed in Renaissance blue and gold.

The ninety year old Mother Superior was kneeling in prayer between two young nuns, while a few pilgrims who had ventured into this inner sanctum crowded round to touch the icons, their lips moving in mute prayer. I hardly dared to breath for fear of disturbing the quietude. Presently, her two companions helped the Mother Superior to stand and led her out, kissing her hands.

Emerging into the afternoon sun was like waking from a disturbing dream, as if time had stopped for a while and suddenly moved again. 'You like it?' asked Qader. I didn't know what to answer – 'like' was not the right word; I was awed.

We drove back to the main road and continued towards Maalula. This small town huddles against the mountain in a cluster of houses – pale blue, honey yellow – above a valley of poplar, walnut and mulberry trees. We stopped in a crowded central square where Qader inevitably had 'one friend' – a Christian baker who sold us delicious oven-hot flat bread on which he spread olive paste and oregano, a local speciality. Until recently, the population of Maalula was mostly Christian, Greek Orthodox or Catholic, and they spoke Aramaic. Centuries before Christ, Aramaic was the dominant tongue of the Middle East, and when Cyrus conquered the region in the

5th Century BC, it became the *lingua franca* of the western provinces of the Persian Empire. Surviving the advent of Islam and the spread of Arabic over the whole region in isolated pockets, it has now all but disappeared, though some in the old villages and monks in the monastery can still speak it.

A steep path led to the Church of St Sergius, built in 7th Century and named after a famous mediaeval saint and martyr. In the courtyard of the monastery, I was greeted by Father Faez – a genial, plump, sweating monk who first offered me a small glass of wine in the souvenir shop. This was a gesture of hospitality extended to all visitors while they made their small purchases of postcards, books and trinkets. Soon the Lebanese group he had been attending departed, and the Father offered to guide me around the church himself – a small, harmonious building flooded with light. He told me that its Byzantine dome had been destroyed and rebuilt as the original, that many parts had been damaged and repaired over the centuries but that the beams were fifteen hundred years old and the oval marble altar the oldest in the world, used for animal sacrifices in the pre-Christian era. There was a baldaquin whose ceiling was painted with moons and stars: 'When we pray, Heaven echoes and joins in our worship.' There were some fine mediaeval icons – the Last Supper, Christ the King, the Virgin. A beautiful one of the three Marys at the Cross had been stolen six months earlier, Father Faez told me. (I hope it has been recovered since.) I wondered if he spoke Aramaic. 'I do,' he said, 'and I will recite the Lord's prayer for you, as a present.' He then stood by the altar, raised his arms in supplication and began, modulating the phrases. The language, a cousin of Hebrew and Arabic, sounded softer and more mellifluous than either. I was moved. This must be how Christ first uttered the prayer to the Disciples, for despite the doubts cast by recent research on the historical accuracy of the Scriptures, it seems that the Lord's

Prayer and the Sermon on the Mount are indeed the words of Christ Himself.

Beyond the monastery, a path led to a cleft in the mountain and the Chapel of St Thekla, carved into the rocks which form an uneven arch over the platform. Water from it drips into an old stone fount all the year round at a slow, regular pace that keeps it half-full. The chapel was closed, but a nun was remoulding used candles under an apricot tree, and she told me the legend of the saint... Thekla of Iconium (now Konya in Turkey) was a ravishing pagan girl converted by St Paul. She broke her engagement to devote her life to God. Her enraged fiancé had her condemned to be burnt to death, but a sudden thunderstorm put the fire out, and she escaped to the mountains. Finding her way barred by the cliffs, she prayed so fervently that a thunderbolt split them and let her through. I told the nun about another saint, buried in Konya, whose mausoleum is also visited by thousands – a 13th Century Persian poet and mystic, Mowlana Jalal al-Din Rumi, founder of the Sufi order now known as the Mevlevi whirling dervishes, and I translated for her some of his verses about Jesus and His 'healing breath', His promise of salvation, ending with:

> Love is that which stuns you,
> And takes you beyond Faith and Doubt.

She was astonished and delighted and asked me to stay in the convent for the night, but I explained that I had to move on. 'Next time,' I said; '*Inshallah* – God willing.'

My storyteller made the sign of the cross on my brow and wished me a safe journey.

As I climbed down from the cliffs, I reflected that it is not only history which lives on in these ancient hidden corners; there are also rich stores of myth and legend accumulated over aeons of longing and faith. Visiting such places puts us in touch with our inner selves and awakens our deeper apprehension of Being, otherwise why would one be leaving with a faint feeling of regret?

The cry of a muezzin came from a distance: '*Allah Akbar,* God is Great!' Here was an example of religious tolerance, people of different faiths living together in harmony, each worshipping God in his own way. 'We are all peoples of the Book,' Qader commented. 'Long may it last,' I murmured in response, for it has not always been thus!

The 210 mile highway from Damascus to Aleppo runs along the western rim of the Fertile Crescent, and Homs is half way between. This intersection of ancient caravan routes is now a lively industrial city – Syria's third, with a population of half-a-million, where pipelines from the oil fields of Iraq and northern Syria converge in a huge refinery. Called Emesa in Roman times, Homs prospered as the staging point for westward-going caravans from Palmyra. It rose to prominence when Julia Domina, a high priest's daughter, married the Roman commander Septimius Severus, who became emperor after a coup in 193. She was a beautiful and spirited girl, who became a patroness of the arts in Rome and a friend of artists and savants of her day, 'at some cost to her chastity', it is said. When Aurelian defeated Queen Zenobia of Palmyra in 272, Homs began to decline. Its fortune rose briefly after the Arab conquest, but it did not really recover until recent industrial times. It is now a dusty, concrete-grey modern town, with little left of its long history except remnants of a mediaeval citadel and a few yards of an Arab city wall. A small museum has recently been established in an Ottoman building, but it was closed.

We drove through the crowded streets to the town's most impressive building, the Mosque and Shrine of Khalid Ibn al-Walid, leader of the Arab forces at the time of the conquest, whom the Prophet lauded as 'the Sword of Islam'. Not far away is the tomb of Amr Ibn Mdi Karb, a poet whose epics inspired the troops. We found the Church of Umm-a-Zunnar (The Virgin's girdle), where a strip of cloth found in 1953 was declared by the Orthodox Church to be that of the Virgin Mary. Qader disappeared to find the caretaker who could show it to me. He was nowhere to be found. 'Not matter,' declared Qader; 'it looks very old and shabby.' So we walked to the 6th Century Church of St Elias, which has been destroyed and rebuilt many times. The murals discovered in its crypt in 1970, depicting Christ, the Virgin, Mary Magdalen and assorted saints, are perhaps the oldest in Christiandom.

Qader was getting restless – it was late afternoon and we had some 25 miles to go before stopping for the night at Hama.

This stretch of road follows the valley of the Orontes, a wide and fertile strip between the mountains and the plain, Syria's main agricultural region. Fields of corn and cotton, sugar beet and barley alternate with vineyards, orchards, pistachio and olive groves. Men, women and children pick fruit in the fields. Urchins line the road, cheering the passing cars and waving handfuls of fresh walnuts. We stopped to buy some; the white fruit shone against the children's black palms like jewels in velvet cases. The green skin of the fruit produces a dark juice which is a fast dye, traditionally used in cloth and carpet weaving. My mind jumped back decades, and I recalled my own hands remaining black for weeks after I had peeled walnuts from a huge tree in our garden in Persia. Qader called out to the little boys to bring us some. We took a handful, and I offered money to pay for it, but they squealed with laughter and ran away, disappearing among the trees. 'They see you are foreign guest,' Qader explained, 'so they don't accept money.' I was moved by their generosity, especially considering how poor they were – little *grands seigneurs* in heart and spirit teaching me a lesson in hospitality.

'We will be in Hama at best time – very cool and nice,' said Qader, accelerating.

Stretching along Western Syria like a wall, the mountains suddenly break at the level of Homs, creating a wide gap – the Homs Gap. In the past, caravans from Palmyra and the East came this way to reach the port of Tartus. Today the country's main oil pipeline and a highway run through it.

Turning west from Homs, we came upon a signpost to Krak des Chevaliers, six miles to the north. Presently it rose from the mountaintop, a giant surveying the surrounding plane – 'the finest castle in the world... the most picturesque I have seen – quite marvellous,' wrote Lawrence of Arabia in 1909. Remarkably well preserved, with some judicious restoration by the French in 1936, it is the supreme example of the Crusaders' military architecture. Controlling the Gap was essential for any ruler of Syria, and there had been an outpost here from the time of the Hittites. But the first fortress was built in 1031 by the Emir of Homs; it was taken by Raymond de Toulouse in 1099 during the First Crusade, retaken once again by Tancred of Antioch a year later and finally destroyed. Today's castle was built by the Knights Hospitaller in 1144 and expanded later by the Mamelukes, who added the moat.

In spite of these vicissitudes, the Krak was virtually impregnable – even Saladin, to whom castles were pawns to a chessboard king, was daunted by its defences and decided against assault. Eventually, after a long, exhausting siege, it was given away in 1271 by the last of the Knights to the Mameluke Sultan Baibar in exchange for safe conduct to Tartus, whence they sailed back to Europe.

A drawbridge over the moat leads to the entrance tower – a vaulted passage that rises steeply and twists at right angles, with openings in the ceiling to let in the sun. Two thousand troops were garrisoned here, fully prepared for months and even years of siege. There were stables for hundreds of horses, baths, kitchens, wells and cisterns, even a prison, and all this made it a self-sufficient miniature city. One can get lost wandering through its towers and passages, until one emerges on the top where the view stretches on all sides over an amazing landscape. In spring and summer the plain is green with vegetation: there are fields of sunflower and maize, vineyards and olive groves and orchards. In autumn and winter cold winds from the sea whirl through the Gap, bringing rain and snow and wrapping the land in thick mist. Now, it being autumn, I was nearly blown off by the wind. I could see to infinity on one side; a pall of cloud covered the rest.

There was no sign of Hama before we reached it, but suddenly there it was, under an escarpment in a wide green valley, with the Orontes meandering through – a hidden haven surrounded by windswept plain. We wound our way to the river bank and settled under a vine trellis in a café on the edge of the water. One of the most beautiful towns in Syria, Hama is particularly famous for its norias – gigantic wheels that raise water from the river and tilt it onto the aqueducts which carry it to the surrounding fields and orchards. They were invented by the Byzantines – a 5th Century mosaic at the National Museum in Damascus depicts a noria on the Orontes, and the present norias are from the Middle Ages. 'I saw a large river… and on its banks observed water-wheels that faced each other. Along these banks are disposed gardens that hang their branches over the water,' wrote the Andalusian traveller Ibn Jubayr in the 12th Century. 'The green leaves look like down on its cheeks as it flows through their shade...' But Hama is much older, its origins going back to the Stone Age. Mentioned in the Book of *Joshua* as Hamath, it traded with the Kingdom of Israel in the reign of King David. Assyrians, Persians, Greeks and Romans conquered it in turn; then it fell to the Arabs.

A breeze swayed the trees along the banks; ducks and swans glided over the water; children swam in the pools round the norias, catching hold of the blades, then riding up and diving down from the top or going all the way round and round as on a Ferris Wheel, disappearing under water and emerging like sprites. 'It is absolutely forbidden to swim,' Qader shook his head. 'That is what children rightly do with silly laws,' I said.

The terrace faced huge norias, slowly turning and moaning and groaning like large clocks lamenting the passage of time. The spray they sent up caught the light of the setting sun, turning each drop into a rainbow.

The café was crowded with Lebanese tourists, families of several generations, from elderly grandparents to toddlers and babies, their tables laden with appetising dishes. By contrast, European tourists were in groups of the same age. It occurred to me that there is something life-affirming in the Oriental mixed assemblies; surrounded by their progeny, the old feel less isolated, seeing in their children and grandchildren a continuation of their own lives – the only immortality we can be sure of. Further along, young men were smoking the nargileh, flicking their beads, talking animatedly. I asked for some watermelon – honey-sweet and thirst-quenching. 'Lebanese girls pretty, more freer than Syrian girls,' observed Qader, casting round expert eyes. 'They have lovely eyes, like Persian women.'

Hama has always been a bastion of religious orthodoxy, and many of the local women are still completely covered in black veils. Qader did not approve: 'Why should men do everything they want, but women no? My son want in marriage, my wife and I go see the girl. We say to him, look, it is not good just see with eyes and say I want that girl; we must see that her family is good, the girl is good, then we give permission. In Europe men leave their wives – not good, very bad, very. I never go with other women, just my wife, even though she is fat and I like thin women, like this,' and he lifted his little finger to show how slim she should be. 'My wife was very slim, but every day become more fatter, and now very big, but her face still pretty.' I told him he should not expect more after ten pregnancies and childbirths and the hard work it entailed. He looked puzzled.

The oldest norias are half-a-mile upstream. From my hotel room I could see a large wheel above a deep pool at a river bend. As night fell, darkness blurred its outline and heightened its plaintive drone, as if the ghosts of a thousand armies had gathered to haunt the city. For Hama has been the scene of many bloody battles in its long history. The last took place in 1982, when the fundamentalist Muslim Brotherhood rose against the secular government of President Assad. In the confrontation that followed the rebellion was ruthlessly quelled, and up to 25,000 died. Qader would not speak about it, but Syrian friends told me the story: 'The fundamentalists would not compromise; when asked what they wanted, they said "Assad's head on a plate". They had already killed many Alawis – the Shia sect to which the President belonged – so the army attacked, from the air and on the land, and destroyed the rebels.' It was a war of attrition, in which many innocents were killed too: 'That soured the population. But apart from that people were not displeased with the outcome, as they did not want a fundamentalist régime, and were relieved to be rid of the Brotherhood.' In the light of what has happened since – the atrocities and massacres perpetrated by the fundamentalists in Egypt and Algeria – one can sympathise with them, while deploring the loss of life. The problem is the absence of democratic institutions that would guarantee against such internecine collisions and bloody feuds.

The war razed many buildings to the ground, including the magnificent al-Nourriyeh Grand Mosque, built in 1172 by Saladin's predecessor, Nureddin. It replaced a Byzantine church, erected on the foundations of a temple of Baal.

In the morning we went for a tour of the city. Only a few fragments are left of a once mighty citadel on top of a hill surrounded by parks, but the view over the whole town is spectacular. The Grand Mosque was closed for repairs, so we drove down to see the Azem Palace, built by the same man whose residence I had seen in Damascus, the one who had been the governor of Hama – his birthplace – before being promoted to the capital. This beautiful 18th Century Ottoman building is a museum now. A tiled courtyard with a fountain at its centre and decorative trees is surrounded with deep open eywans (verandas), which enabled the household to enjoy an outdoor life within the privacy of the palace. A second courtyard on the first-floor has a charming view over the river, while inside the rooms are frescoed with sylvan scenery. We skipped the bazaar – 'best bazaar in Aleppo,' Almighty decreed – but quickly visited the town's most famous caravanserai. The Khan Rustem Pasha was built in 1556 and named after Suleiman the Magnificent's vizir, who married his favourite daughter, Princess Mehrima. There are many more mosques and residences worthy of a glimpse, but we pressed on to Aleppo.

Thirty miles west of Hama lie the ruins of Apamea, a city founded by Seleucus I Nicator, one of Alexander's generals, in the 3rd Century BC, and named after his Persian wife. It became an important military and trading point and the favourite city of the Seleucid rulers. They grazed their 30,000 horses and trained their eight hundred war-elephants in the surrounding pastures, while the town itself flourished and became the heart of a new Macedonia. After Apamea fell to the Romans in 64 BC, they gradually rebuilt it in their own style, and today's ruins date from 2nd Century AD. A whole new city grew here during the Middle Ages, including a citadel, Qalat Mudhig, destroyed in turn by earthquakes and wars. The Ottomans added their own contribution of mosques and khans and hammams.

Almighty left me to fend for myself, saying that he would drive around the town, see some friends and meet me at the other end of the ruined Apamea. 'But first we must see the museum in the village,' he said. This is a 16th Century Ottoman caravanserai – a vast sun-bleached courtyard surrounded by cool vaulted halls. They house some sculptures and capitals from Greek and Byzantine periods, while the floors are covered with fine mosaics, their subjects ranging from Adam and St Paul to Aphrodite and Socrates, the latter dating from the 4th Century when Apamea became a centre of Neo-Platonism.

The view from the citadel spreads over the whole region, and the Roman city in the foreground gives an idea of its layout and scale: a cardo maximus – a grand colonnaded avenue from the reign of Marcus Aurelius in the 2nd Century – a nymphaeum, an agora and a temple of Zeus. There were no other visitors, indeed not a soul in the ghost town, and wandering alone among the ruins under the midday sun, I could conjure up the city at the height of its glory, the lines of shops behind the colonnade, the chariots driving along the wide avenues, the women at the fountain, the commotion at the intersections. Presently, a young man appeared as if from nowhere, smiling at my surprise. Lean and dark, with jet-black eyes glinting in the sun: 'Look, lady, I have coins, real antiques, I dig them myself here, cheap for you.' He opened a handkerchief and showed me a dozen coins and a tiny bronze statuette. I asked him how he could find them when it was forbidden for anyone except archaeologists to work on the site. 'I come at night when the moon shine and nobody there.' As we talked, I heard the vroom of a motorcycle, and the young man jumped over the stones and vanished like a lizard, leaving me wondering whether he had been a figment of the imagination. The motorcycle figure shimmering in the haze turned out to be the curator and guardian of the site, who had come to warn me against false antique dealers: 'It is all fake; don't buy anything from them. They are barred from here by law, but they still come.' He gave me a bumpy, bone-shattering ride through the ruins, explaining the columns and the carvings and telling me about recent excavations and restorations. I hadn't enjoyed a motorcycle ride as much, nor been so scared, since my student days in Paris. Qader was waiting at the far end, and we drove on to Aleppo, his home town. 'Aleppo even more beautiful than Damascus, you'll see.'

The traffic on the highway swelled as we approached Aleppo: lorries full of fruit and vegetables, buses and cars bursting with passengers, cyclists alarmingly dodging their way in and out of the lanes. Presently, the city appeared, spread below in an oval bowl with its citadel rising on a mound in the middle. Aleppo's Arabic name is Halab – milk. It is based on the legend that Abraham milked his cattle here to feed the poor and prayed on the summit of the hill where the citadel stands. Aleppo's origins go back to the Hittites, who were followed by the Assyrians and the Persians, before Alexander the Great conquered the town in 333 BC. It fell to Pompey in 64 BC and remained in Roman – later Byzantine – hands until the Arab conquest in 637 AD.

During the centuries that followed, Aleppo's fortunes fluctuated. Saladin captured it from the Crusaders and appointed his son al-Zaher Ghazi its governor, and the town prospered. Then came the Mongol invasion in the 13th Century and its destruction by Tamerlane in 1400. Finally, in 1516, the Ottomans arrived and stayed until the end of World War I.

An Aleppan Greek wrote an itinerary which ended up here after starting in China. Aleppo's prosperity has always depended on trade; the mythical Silk Road invented by modern travel writers is based on the Greek's document. Under the Ottomans, Aleppo flourished, becoming the third most important trade centre in the Levant, after Constantinople and Smyrna. Great caravanserais were built; there merchants from the East exchanged textiles and gems and spices for sacks of gold and silver. When in 1517 Soleiman the Magnificent consented to treat with strangers, François I of France opened a consulate in one of the khans. It was the first in the world. Three years later, the Venetians built a consulate in the town's most beautiful caravanserai – the only one which is still inhabited. In 1581 Queen Elizabeth I founded the Levant Company, and the English set up their own trading house. Aleppo is mentioned in *Macbeth* and *Othello*.

I had two days in a city which deserves at least a week. It is stuffed with history, and its bazaar is second only to Istanbul's. Qader knew every nook and cranny of it and seemingly all the inhabitants too; there were greetings and embraces at every stop, and as I like wandering on my own, I sometimes left him with his friends and joined him later.

I started with the Museum of Archaeology, with exhibits from the Iron Age to the Islamic period: gigantic statues from the 9th Century BC in black basalt with menacing white eyes greet you at the entrance, while inside Greek and Roman statuary and mosaics, Islamic faïence and glassware, pottery and coins mark the stages of Aleppo's long history. Next we went to the citadel, whose foundations go back to 1000 BC; it became Ghazi's residence in the 12th Century, was nearly destroyed by Tamerlane and repaired in the following centuries, while the city grew and spread all around it. The bridge over the moat is sixty feet wide and one hundred feet long; it leads to an awe-inspiring entrance befitting the scale and grandeur of the edifice. The palaces and mosques and other structures inside were built and rebuilt by successive rulers: the Mosque of Abraham, Ghazi's Great Mosque of the Citadel, the remains of the Barracks. Finally, I emerged to a grand view over the town and had a rest at the café on the terrace before clambering down to my next destination, the Great Mosque, which was built by the Umayyads a decade after its counterpart in Damascus. It has similar arcades around its court; inside the prayer hall, next to the fine carved mimbar, a reliquary, covered with embroidered cloth of gold, is believed to contain the head of Zacharia, the father of St John the Baptist.

Qader was anxious to take me to the bazaar, with its original stone vaulted ceiling. Walking through a maze of souks, we caught the smells of saffron and cinnamon and attar and reached the goldsmiths' souk, where the shops and booths cheek-by-jowl glittered with a tangle of gold bangles and chains, rings and plates of precious stones, creating a dream-like vision. Qader led me to 'one friend's' shop where we drank coffee and bargained, and I finally bought a small anklet. 'Good price, cheaper for you,' Qader reassured me afterwards.

Of the city's dozens of madrassahs, mosques, caravanserais and hammams, we could only visit a few. The serene 13th Century Madrassah Firdows, 'the School of Paradise,' was founded by Daifeh Khanum, Saladin's niece and daughter-in-law; the 12th Century Madrassah Halawiyeh was erected on the foundations of a cathedral dedicated to St Helena, the mother of Constantine; the 16th Century Khan al-Nahasin – the coppersmiths – was built by the Venetians, while across the courtyard you find the oldest inhabited house in Aleppo, which until recently was occupied by the Belgian Consul. The 12th Century Hammam al-Nahasin was closed to women, but Qader enthused about it.

In the evening, I asked Qader to drive to the legendary Baron Hotel, which used to be the most famous in town. The two Mazloumian brothers, Armenian refugees from Turkey, who opened it in 1909, have long gone, but their descendants still run the hotel. Built in a green residential part on the edge of town, it was hailed as the first hotel in Syria to combine Western comfort with Eastern hospitality, personal service with delicious cooking – pheasants shot in the neighbouring countryside, Persian caviar, venison and wild boar and vintage French wines. Today its white facade and curved, ivy-clad balconies stand out amid a welter of concrete buildings. Inside, it has the haunting charm of a vanished age, when the Orient Express from Europe to Baghdad via Constantinople stopped in Aleppo for the travellers to stay at the hotel.

The Baron's long list of famous past guests is headed by T. E. Lawrence. He first arrived at the hotel in the autumn of 1909, a 21 year old Oxford undergraduate, after a walk of about twelve hundred miles across Palestine, Lebanon and Syria, visiting the Crusaders' castles. Soon he returned to work on an archaeological dig and in 1917, as we know, led the Arab Revolt which put an end to the Ottoman Empire. Lawrence memorabilia – photos, bills and letters – are on show in the hotel lounge. Other guests included Agatha Christie, who accompanied her archaeologist husband and wrote *Murder On the Orient Express* here. (She was once asked who would make the best husband: 'An archaeologist,' she replied, 'the older you get, the more he will love you.') And there were Ataturk, Lindbergh, Theodore Roosevelt and many more.

We sat in deep leather armchairs in the bar and ordered fresh lemonade. Outside the dusk gathered; the lights came on in the garden among the trees, and traffic rumbled past. I told Qader that the next time I came to Syria I might stay at the Baron.

'*Inshallah!*' he said.

We had dinner at Sissi House, a 17th Century residence turned into a restaurant serving Aleppan specialities. Its carved and painted ceilings and panelling have been restored and its balconies made into pergolas. Nearby we came upon Beyt Wakil, another Ottoman house, which now belongs to the Orthodox Church; it was being converted into a hotel. The inauguration was to take place a few days later, and workmen were labouring overtime on the finishing touches. Mr Habib, the enthusiastic manager, showed me around: 'The house is 450 years old. It was built after Tamerlane destroyed the town. We have only twelve rooms and three suites. The rooms round the small courtyard have stone walls, high ceilings and cupolas, and the largest rooms have become the lobby and restaurant ('Best cooking in Aleppo!') – and the wooden furniture is copied from the original. We are already fully booked for months,' Mr. Habib was glad to say, kindly adding, 'but you come and stay as my guest.'

Aleppo has a large Christian population – Maronites, Orthodox, Catholics, Armenians and many more, with their own churches, mostly in Jadayda, the Christian quarter to the north of the city. It is a picturesque bit which grew up during the Ottoman era, and contains some elegant houses built by rich 17th and 18th Century Christian merchants. We wandered through cobbled lanes flanked by stone houses with arched entryways, heavy studded doors and upper stories that overhang the street. In the Armenian part, the old wooden facades and wrought-iron balconies have survived. The Beyt Ajiqbash, an 18th Century residence of a Christian merchant of the same name, is now the Museum of Popular Traditions. Its tree-lined courtyard, with fountain in the middle, has beautiful carvings and a large eywan. In the grand reception room, with a ceiling of splendid painted woodwork and carved panelling on the walls, old furniture and dummies in obsolete stately clothes recall the daily life of a prosperous family of past time. Nearby, a 15th Century Gregorian Armenian church is the oldest in the quarter; it houses some remarkable icons, mostly by 17th Century masters of the Aleppo School. The Armenians are the largest Christian group, refugees from persecution in Turkey having doubled their number between 1894 and 1915. Yet Syria was a vilayet of the Ottoman Empire, which indicates the easygoing organisation of its colonies – a group that was persecuted in one province could find refuge in another. Ottoman dominions ran their own internal affairs and were left alone, as long as they did not rebel and paid their taxes.

Having an introduction to the French-speaking novelist Myriam Antaki and her husband Georges, an eminent businessman and Honorary Consul of Italy and Portugal, I was in luck. Their house, a 19th Century Ottoman building, is famous for being the most beautiful in Aleppo and, indeed, is one of the loveliest I have ever seen anywhere. It is hard to fit in sudden arrivals from abroad, but the hospitable Antakis had me for drinks that evening, and we sat in a ravishing garden under a pistachio tree laden with ripe fruit, the air filled with the scent of jasmine and citrus and eucalyptus. The outer wall was entirely covered with Virginia creeper, while opposite a long portico housed beautiful 2nd Century mosaics and marble busts of Roman women. I recalled Baudelaire's 'La vie antérieure':

> *J'ai longtemps habité sous de vastes portiques*
> *Que les soleils marins teignaient de mille feux...*

The Antakis are keen collectors, and their house is full of wonderful objects, many of them unique, that they have discovered and assembled over the years. Yet it does not feel like a museum but has a lived-in, cheerful and welcoming atmosphere. It is always full of guests, many of whom arrive with only a tenuous introduction but, when they leave, feel like lifelong friends, as I did.

❧

The highlands north of Aleppo are strewn with the ruins of towns and villages known as 'The Dead Cities', some dating back to Greek and Roman times, others to the early Byzantine period. Of these ruins the best preserved and most interesting single instance is Qalat Samaan – The Church of St Simeon, 25 miles northwest of Aleppo, perched upon a hill above the small town of Deir Samaan.

The new asphalt road we took ran through an arid landscape relieved by patches of cultivation – fields of okra and corn, olive groves and orchards. Here and there a cluster of new buildings appeared, a flag flapping above the police station. A little girl in a red dress ran from a house to wave at the car; an old man sat behind a mound of watermelons on the edge of the road; a slow heavily-laden donkey lurched along, ignoring the traffic. Soon we reached the entrance of the site, where we sat in a café and ordered Turkish coffee. From a mound of watermelons on sale I bought a huge one to share with three students from England, the only other visitors.

St Simeon the Stylite was born in 386. At the age of sixteen, he joined a monastery in Mount Hermon and a decade later moved to the place now known as Deir Samaan. He seems to have had a penchant for extreme discomfort: he starved himself nearly to death each Lent, lived for long periods in a well and at one point even buried himself up to his neck in the monastery garden. Still not satisfied, he finally retreated to the top of a pillar, where he spent his last 38 years, regardless of the burning sun in summer and the winter's icy winds and bitter snows. He gradually increased the height of his pillar until it reached sixty feet. A chain fastened him to it in case he dozed off at night, and his brother monks occasionally carried him some food up a ladder. His fame spread, and pilgrims came from as far afield as Constantinople and England to see him, hear him preach and celebrate mass from the top of his pillar. But he had no truck with adulation and in particular would allow no woman near him. Ironically, the village of Deir Samaan was then called Telanissos – the Mountain of Women. His eccentricity caught on, and for a while Stylites appeared all over the Byzantine world, though none achieved St Simeon's legendary reputation, and none was canonised – perhaps the Church decided that one eccentric was enough – and the fashion died out.

A huge basilica was built after Simeon's death in 459 around his *stylos*, of which only the base now remains. It consists of four octagons in the shape of a cross. Though the domes have gone, the pillars and arches and intricate carvings and mouldings give an idea of the beauty and grandeur of what was then the largest church in the world. To the left of it is a square baptistry, where catechumens were baptised in a sunken font. From here, a magnificent view spreads over the village of Deir Samaan: a swarm of bee-coloured flat roofs huddle against the hillside, and the broad green valley is watered by the river Afrin. On the horizon is the shadow of hills and the Turkish frontier beyond – 25 miles.

As we walked among the ruins, I marvelled at the faith and the devotion of those who spent their lives building such fares – the army of stone-masons, carvers and plasterers – until the pillars rose to heaven and the domes curved over them and the doors were hinged to enclose the sacred space, *ad majorem dei gloriam*. A motif on a stone sarcophagus contained the Greek letters Alpha and Omega – the Beginning and End: 'Some people don't believe in second life after this one,' Qader remarked, 'but I do. What meaning has life if there is nothing after? God would not create a world without meaning.'

'You must to my house for dinner,' Almighty insisted. So we drove back towards Aleppo and took a dusty by-road to his village. All around was flat, reddish earth, reclaimed here and there for olives and pomegranate trees or small allotments of vegetables. The villages through which we passed consisted of new limestone houses: 'Before, no buildings here – people were Bedouins, lived in tents. My grandfather was a Bedouin, came from Yemen; he build the first house. Now six hundred people live in village. I bring the water-man before I buy the land, and he go round with a stick looking at earth until he find water. So I dig the well where he say, and water jump up.' Qader had planted a cypress and a palm, several olive and pomegranate trees, and surrounded his property with a stone wall. Chickens and ducks pecked about under the trees; a cat was half asleep beside the well. The house itself consisted of two rooms and a wide veranda supported by four columns, one of which was covered with jasmine.

Qader collected some of the fallen petals in a plate and brought it to me. Again my mind jumped back several decades, and I saw my father collecting jasmine petals in a blue bowl and bringing it to my mother, who was sitting by the samovar at the breakfast table under a vine trellis in our garden. Now we sat on a rug in the veranda; a cloth was spread while Qader's wife and pretty, slim daughter brought in the meal – delicious stuffed vegetables and lamb stew. 'My daughter is sixteen, and she will be in marriage next month. The boy good – I know his family.' My heart sank at the thought of her growing stout and middle-aged with endless pregnancies before she had enjoyed her youth. 'No more than two!' I said to her mother, lifting two fingers. She spread her hand to indicate ten! We laughed. 'She want another baby herself, but I say no, ten enough.'

Before I left, Qader's wife presented me with a jar of rose-petal jam – it was my favourite in childhood, and I had almost forgotten it. I said I would use it very sparingly, and share it only with special guests.

The road from Homs to Palmyra cuts a straight line through a bleached, stony wilderness covered with thorn bushes, stretching to infinity. Here and there small flocks of sheep graze on tufts of spiky grass; a tree stands solitary on the edge of a dry channel; black Bedouin tents relieve the dun monotone. Presently, we leave the road and follow the tyre marks of a lorry for a few hundred yards to a Bedouin settlement. Women and children in colourful traditional clothes and headgear rush forward to greet us. 'The men are away with the flocks,' Qader explains, but soon the head of the family arrives – not on a camel as I expected, but in a Mercedes van – and invites us into the largest tent, which is the family's drawing-room. Cushions are produced against which to recline, and we are invited to lunch. Freshly-baked bread and plates of steaming fried aubergine and tomatoes are brought and placed before us.

Apparently these Bedouins are all related, cousins usually marrying cousins, but our host is the only man with two wives: one lives in Homs to look after the children who go to school there, the other is here – a tall, handsome woman with a gold tooth and kohl-black eyes. Some of the younger women's husbands are with the army and come home every few months to see their families – often enough, judging by the swarm of children and babies.

We talk about changing times, the difficulty of earning a living from old style animal husbandry and the recent scarcity of rain. The women ask me about my family, what London is like – 'as big as Homs?' – whether I like Syria and would I settle down there with them. Qader translates it all, and sometimes they hoot with laughter, displaying gold and silver teeth. Eventually we have to leave, and I promise to send them copies of the photographs I have taken.

Palmyra appears on the horizon, like a mirage shimmering in the haze. Called by the Greeks and the Romans 'the place of palms', the oasis was known to its inhabitants as Tadmor and is mentioned in the Bible as one of the cities built by King Solomon in the wilderness. A stop on the caravan route to the East, Palmyra developed into an important city, resisting the predatory ambitions of its powerful neighbours, Persia and Rome, playing one against the other and maintaining a balance of power between them. Yet by the time of Hadrian's visit in 130 AD, Palmyra had become part of the Roman Empire, though retaining a measure of autonomy. The Palmyrians celebrated his arrival with a week of festivities, and in return he bestowed upon their oasis the title of Hadriana and the status of a Free City. In 260 Emperor Valerian was defeated by the Persians (the event is commemorated in a frieze near Persepolis depicting Valerian prostrate before Shapur I), and he later died in captivity. Meanwhile Palmyra's governor, Odaenathus, and his son, fighting for the Romans in Mesopotamia, were assassinated, allegedly by Odaenathus's ambitious wife Zenobia.

She proceeded to win over the army, conquer Egypt, take Antioch and seize part of Asia Minor. Emperor Aurelian, doubtless charmed by her dusky beauty – compared to Cleopatra's by Gibbon – tolerated her behaviour until she declared independence, calling herself Augusta, 'Queen of the East'. She had gone too far: Aurelian fought and defeated her, and she was taken to Rome and paraded through the streets in gold chains. She spent the rest of her life in a villa at Tivoli.

Zenobia's six-year reign was the Golden Age of Palmyra, and her ghost still haunts its ruins, as well as the imagination of historians and writers. (My new friend Myriam Antaki told me that her new historical novel was about Zenobia.) Walking along the street of columns, I could see her driving in her chariot, amidst the cheers of her subjects, dazzling in silk from China, gems from India and pearls from the Persian Gulf, redolent of attar of roses from Isfahan. 'Ah, if they only knew what a woman I have been fighting!' said Aurelian when the Senate mocked him for his victory over a mere woman. 'What would history say if I had been defeated?'

The Roman city whose remnants I had come to see was built over a hundred years after Hadrian's visit, but after its apogee in the 3rd Century it fell into a decline, though the Byzantines added several churches to it and the Umayyads two palaces. It was rediscovered in the 17th Century by European travellers, who found a few Bedouin families living in mud huts among the ruins; but it was not until the 20th Century that excavations were undertaken, first by Western archaeologists and later by the Syrians themselves. The mud huts were removed and the families settled in the adjoining town of Tadmor.

Jamal, a young history graduate and friend of Qader's, joined us as a guide, and we started at the Temple of Bel, which stands on high ground and dominates the city. Consecrated in 32 AD in the reign of Tiberius, it was dedicated to the Aramean god Bel – Master, or Creator of the World – later identified with Baal, Zeus and Jupiter. The temple is at the centre of a vast rectangle surrounded by walls, with a double row of tall, graceful Corinthian columns forming a gallery around it. The cella – inner sanctum – has two chambers at either end, covered with monolithic carved stones, which contained effigies of gods, in particular a statue of Bel, used in religious procession. Bel was the Lord of Heavens, and stairs from these chambers led to the roof for special rituals involving communion with the stars, while the central cupola featured the planets and signs of the Zodiac. The cella was surrounded by forty slim columns with gilded capitals, of which only a few remain. 'Imagine how the gold glittered at night, like a lighthouse in the desert darkness, guiding the caravans,' said Jamal. The remains of a sacrificial altar near the cella indicate that ritual sacrifices of animals took place in the temple: 'The high priest would kill the animals, which were cooked and served to guests in the refectory behind.'

To the west of the temple, a processional way led to a triumphal arch and street of columns, the main artery of the town. Today the highway from Damascus to Tadmor runs through it, heavy lorries threatening the arch with their vibrations. 'Before it was just camels,' says Jamal ruefully. Time and sand have eroded the columns, particularly around their bases. Many have protruding platforms two-thirds up, on which stood statues of dignitaries. Walking along the colonnade, the plan of the town and its various landmarks emerge: the remains of a temple of Nabo, the Babylonian god identified with Apollo; the four monolithic pink columns of the Baths of Diocletian, hauled here from Aswan in Egypt; traverse streets leading to a theatre and an agora.

We emerged from the mile-long street and drove up the hill

to the remains of a 17th Century fortress on the summit. It was the magical hour: the sun setting on the horizon, the ruined city bathed in a golden glow, the palms casting long shadows on the sand, the gardens and orchards of the oasis of Tadmor flickering with coloured lights. To my left was a silhouette of hills, to my right desolation stretching out of sight. Below the hills I could see the Valley of the Tombs: four or five storey towers where the dead were either buried or stacked in niches. They show the influence of Zoroastrian funerary towers: the Palmyrians, notably in their clothes and ornaments, absorbed many things of Persian life.

Jamal invited me to see his house. It had a balcony over-looking the Roman site, and he was converting it into a small hotel, named after Emperor Caracalla: 'Only two rooms for special guests; best food, omelettes with truffles I find myself in the desert. You must stay here next time.' We sat on his balcony drinking lemonade and watching the shadows deepen and sky turn indigo, until darkness swallowed the scene, and I left Jamal to his thoughts.

Before leaving early the next morning, we went for a tour of Tadmor. The little bazaar was full of Bedouins in their proper clothes – the women in embroidered caftans and fringed scarves, their faces tattooed, their eyes emphasised with kohl; the men in loose jellabas. Local knickknacks abounded.

Many of the finds in Palmyra have been moved to the Museum of Archaeology in Damascus. But in the Palmyra Museum, I saw some funerary statues from the Tombs. Buried in the sand for centuries, they had been safe from theft and were in good condition. Their elaborately embroidered and jewel-encrusted clothes show the Sassanian influence, while the simpler garments indicate a preference for the Roman fashion.

The domestic life of more recent times is illustrated at a new Museum of Popular Culture. In a town house and a Bedouin tent, furnished in old desert style, hand-spun rugs, dressed mannequins, caparisoned camels and stuffed desert fauna bear witness to a way of life that used to captivate English travellers. Among them were Lady Hester Stanhope, who came to Palmyra in 1813 and stayed on to become known as the 'Queen of the Desert'; also Lady Jane Digby, who, after being mistress to, among others, Ludwig I of Bavaria and Honoré de Balzac, married a sheikh seventeen years her junior and lived happily ever after in a tent in Palmyra.

'There was gazelle and panther in the desert before,' says Qader as we leave the town. 'Now all gone.' Overpopulation and tourism will destroy what remains, unless something is done. It is the same conflict between development and conservation as all over the Third World.

Along the road to Damascus, eagles and kestrels wheel in the sky, and hundreds of sparrows and larks settle on the asphalt and fly off as the car approaches: 'The asphalt glitter in the sun and the birds think it is water, so they come down to drink,' comments Qader. 'We call the shiny bits "lark's mirror",' I say, 'meaning it is an illusion, not real.' He shakes his head: 'Life full of that.'

It was my last day. Qader and I set off early for Bosra, seventy miles south of Damascus in Hauran, a fertile region that slopes gradually towards the Jebel al-Arab (formerly Jebel Druze). It rises to six thousand feet. In the Bible, it was coveted and won by the Egyptians and the Persians before being absorbed into the Roman Empire. Its black lava soil and heavy rain made it an important source of food for the Empire, and even today it is one of the richest part of Syria, producing wheat, barley, cotton, tobacco, sweet wines and marvellous fruit. The road was lined with trestles of melons, pistachios and walnuts, and a troop of men and women were picking fruit in the orchards. Qader stopped the car, disappeared for a few minutes and came back wit a big bowl of golden figs. 'These good because they get no water after the winter rains. If you water fig trees after that, the fruit become less sweet,' Almighty knew. 'The farmer next door water his orchard, so his figs are bigger but less delicious.'

Soon we reached Shahba, the birthplace of the 3rd Century Emperor Philip, known as Philip the Arab. The town was built by the Romans and girdled with a wall; then it declined and gradually crumbled away. It was discovered in 1810 by Johann Burckhardt, the explorer who found Petra. Later it was settled by the Druze, who built their own homes among the ruins. Distinguished by costume – long flowing skirts, tight bodices and elaborate head-dresses for the women, and a turban and scarf for the men – the Druze belong to a hermetic Islamic sect which goes back to the 12th Century. Romantic Europeans believe that they are descended from the Crusaders, Dreux in particular, hence their white skin, blue eyes and fair hair. But some believe that they came from neighbouring Persia.

The Roman crossroads is now the town's roundabout, and from here the broad main street, still paved with its original flagstones, leads to a wide flight of steps and four huge black basalt columns which form the entrance to the temple. You can see the whole town from the roof – the Roman amphitheatre, the baths and the houses of the new town. Walking along the street to the town museum, I was beckoned by a Druze woman into her tiny house. It was like a closet and almost entirely filled with a loom; there a man was working on a blue kelim with white stripes, which is a favourite local pattern. All around him were bags of wool in primary colours and, on the side, a stack of kelims in various sizes. A few doors further along, another woman asked me to see the inside of *her* minuscule habitat; it had its original Roman stone ceiling and was filled with stacks of tinted straw, which she weaves into baskets of many different designs. Further up, a notary asked us into his office, a square, bare room with a carpet and a few chairs. We drank bitter coffee while our host shared a nargileh with Qader, who translated bits of their conversation – mostly more offers of hospitality and food and enquiries about my country and family. I was struck by the contrast between the hard black mineral – it gave the town a rather dour appearance – and the cheerful, welcoming disposition of its inhabitants.

There are columns and statues and huge olive pots in the museum, but its chief draw lies in the beautiful mosaics. They were discovered on the floor of a house built at the time of Constantine in 330 AD and depict the wedding of Dionysus and Ariadne; Orpheus putting animals under a spell with his lyre; sea-creatures surrounding the goddess Tethys; Ares leading Aphrodite to bed ('Come and lie beside me, my darling, and be happy,' wrote Homer) and the Three Graces.

We drove on to Bosra through a fertile plain strewn with black rocks like whales turned to stone. Once an important point on the routes of pilgrimage and trade, Bosra is now famous for its ancient remains. It has the best preserved Roman amphitheatre in the world. The town's name first appears in 1300 BC, in Egyptian records, but it became prominent under the Romans in the 2nd Century AD, when Trajan stationed his Third Legion there. Later, Philip the Arab raised it to the rank of metropolis. Thereafter its fate was the same as the rest of the country – Byzantium followed by Islam, the Crusades, the Mongols and finally the Ottomans.

The Roman amphitheatre is inside a fort built by the

Umayyads, to which were added nine towers and a deep moat in the 13th Century. A long bridge slopes over the moat to a great gateway and dim entrance hall. From here we were guided by arrows through a labyrinth of dark, twisting passages, up to the top of steep stone stairs and then out into the light. We were standing on the last row of the amphitheatre. Preserved under centuries of sand blown from the desert, it has been carefully restored. The 37 rows of basalt seats are arranged in a semicircle, which is divided by two flights of stairs leading down to a large paved courtyard in front of the stage. It seated an audience of fifteen hundred, and the acoustics are so perfect that even those seated in the top row could hear every syllable clearly. The stage is embellished with slim columns and the facade with coloured marble and statuary. Was the theatre used for drama or gladiatorial games, I wondered, as I noticed the vomitoria either side of the stage. Perhaps both. I was alone; so I stood before the stage and sang a scale which echoed many times before fading away to join all the echoes of the past.

At the café in the piazza outside the citadel we had coffee and kebabs, then walked to the nymphaeum with its four Corinthian columns, equalling in beauty of execution the finest in Baalbek and Palmyra, as Burkhardt said. Nearby we found the recently rescued Roman baths, one of many of which only the scars remain. Once a palatial 2nd Century pile with a colonnaded portico, domed hall and hot and cold chambers, it is now derelict but being restored.

According to a legend, in 581, when the future Prophet of Islam was a twelve year old orphan, he travelled to Syria with his uncle's caravan, and in Bosra he met a Nestorian monk called Bahira. Impressed by his intellectual precocity, the monk predicted a radiant future for him, seeing the 'Seal of Prophesy' between his shoulders. Thereafter Bosra was held in esteem and affection by Muslims and became an important stop on the road to Mecca. Vestiges of Bosra's Islamic past abound, and Qader guided me to a few significant ones.

The Mosque of Omar, built by the second caliph after he had conquered Syria in 636, is supposed, after Mecca and Medina, to be the third oldest in the Islamic world. It was enlarged in the 12th Century and has recently been renovated and reopened. Clearly, old stones from the ruins were used, as some bear Greek inscriptions. A corrugated iron roof now covers the arcaded courtyard, and inside the nave there are fine columns and carvings. More moving is the Mosque of Mabrak, where the Prophet's camel is believed to have knelt for him to dismount. (In a less romantic legend, the camel was merely carrying the first bound copy of the Holy Koran.) The spot is now the mihrab of the mosque, which became a place of pilgrimage; in the 12th Century a madrassah was built next to it, and theology students flocked there from all over Syria.

Saladin and his successors built several other theological schools and many public baths to serve students and pilgrims alike. The most impressive, with its black-and-white ablaq decoration, is the 14th Century Hammam Mnajak. It had eleven hot and cold chambers and enough room for five hundred customers at a time.

The Byzantines' contribution to Bosra was mostly in the form of churches, now dilapidated, and a cathedral, which was dedicated in 512 and was among the earliest in Syria. The dome and walls were standing until the 19th Century, then they fell down; but now the apse and its adjoining chapels are being rebuilt. To the north of this structure are the remains of a 3rd Century basilica, which 'the natives call Deir Bahir', after the Christian monk who was tutor to the Prophet.

One could spend several days exploring Bosra, but I had only one, and as the sun began to go down we headed back to

Damascus. 'I sad you go,' said Almighty, 'you must come back and stay a month in my house.' 'I should like that very much,' I answered sincerely and reflected that I had barely touched the surface of all there was to see and learn in this ancient land. I had enjoyed the exploration, but if anyone asked me what I most appreciated in Syria, I would say the people. They are deeply hospitable and warm-hearted and full of humour and spirit. How long will they remain so? I hope forever. Meanwhile, I remembered a saying attributed to the Prophet Mohammad: 'Joy to the people of Syria, for the angels of merciful God spread their wings over them.'

LEBANON

The Fountain of Adonis

*I pray thee, let me go over, and see the good land
that is beyond Jordan, that goodly mountain,
and Lebanon.*

– Deuteronomy (iii, 25)

Beirut is rising from the ashes of a long civil war. Although
the conflagration engulfed the whole of Lebanon, Beirut
was the epicentre, and two-thirds of it were destroyed. A frenzy
of building began as soon as the guns were finally silenced in
1991. Since then many of the old buildings have been put up
again, and countless new ones have risen everywhere, turning
the city into a forest of cement and glass. Beirut is a gigantic
building site bristling with cranes and scaffolding, and it will be
many years before the work is completed.

I first visited Beirut in the early 1970s, when it was the play-
ground and business centre of the Middle East. Its unique
setting, varied population and frenchified allure – grand hotels,
elegant boutiques, restaurants and night clubs – made it 'the
Paris of the East', while its free port and tolerant rules attracted
business adventurers from all over the world. Millions of petro-
dollars changed hands every night at the Casino, and multi-
national deals were clinched at its exclusive Golf Club and
Sporting Club. 'There were around one hundred banks, nearly

half of them foreign,' Lebanese friends told me; 'during the war they were the only buildings to be spared by the warring factions, as both sides needed them.'

It all came to an end when civil war broke out in 1974. The visitors found new haunts of pleasure; the foreign businessmen took their investments elsewhere; even the Lebanese entrepreneurs left, with their flair and energy, for more propitious climes. The city became an inferno of strife and attrition.

Today business is flourishing again. Many Lebanese entrepreneurs who left during the civil war have returned and brought Western partners and new investors with them. The seafront is tightly packed with new luxury hotels, restaurants and cafés, while the old grand hotels which used to be the rendezvous of local plutocrats and the international jet-set – the St Georges, the Phoenicia, the Vendôme and the Bristol – have been rebuilt. The Casino has recently reopened, and the exclusive Golf and Sporting Clubs are again full.

Healing the collective psyche and repairing the ruined infrastructure is another matter; but the process has started. My Shia Muslim driver, Salman, and my Maronite Christian guide, Jocelyne, aged respectively 21 and 23, grew up during the civil war that decimated their communities; but now they work together and are friends. Indeed, they denied that there had ever been a *civil* war, rather it was a *proxy* war – between America and the Soviet Union, with the connivance of their corrupt clients in the region. But I remembered the poet Christpher Logue's words:

> *All dreams are one dream;*
> *All wars are civil wars.*

There seems to be no bitterness among the young, and once again Muslim, Christians of many denominations and the Druze all live together in peace, though cynics ask 'for how long?'

Meanwhile there is virtually no public transport in Beirut, only cars, which result in a 24 hour traffic jam. As the postal service is unreliable, to say the least, everyone has a portable telephone or communicates by fax. Nevertheless, the atmosphere is vibrant with new energy and willingness, and people seem cheerful.

I spent the first couple of days merely walking around, remembering, identifying old landmarks and breaking new ground. As he drove us to the middle of the town, Salman pointed south: 'That is Shatila, where I was born. I never go there now,' he said sadly, as if trying to banish the memory. The scene of a notorious massacre in 1982 during the Israeli occupation, Sabra and Shatila are now warrens of slums overcrowded with refugees, mainly Palestinians and some Shias from the South. At school, Salman had been a keen student, 'always top of the class', and he wanted to go to university and become a teacher or a doctor. Instead, he had to take a job as a driver to help his father, also a driver, to support their large family. He learnt English from books and by talking to tourists. He wanted to help his younger siblings go to university and break the cycle of poverty in their family. He has a beautiful face, with sad dark eyes, and the expression of premature knowledge of a ruthless world.

By contrast, Jocelyne was educated at a French convent school, learnt French and English, travelled and trained to be a guide; she is attractive, vivacious, efficient and seemed to enjoy life. Both Salman and Jocelyne had strong political views, and while we were travelling around, I realised that, given the state of the country, it was impossible to avoid the subject of politics altogether: the memory of war was still fresh, the Syrian Army ubiquitous, the Israeli Army still in the south and hundreds of thousands of Palestinian refugees in camps.

Driving through the country in the following days, we saw everywhere enlarged photographs of President Assad of Syria, Lebanon's President and Prime Minister and pictures of the Hezbollah leaders and martyrs. In the Middle East, no one is merely a tragic casualty of armed conflict; every death is a martyrdom in a righteous cause and holy war. The title of 'martyr' denies the essential absurdity of war, confers dignity on the victims, ennobles their actions and comforts the bereaved. I thought of their mothers, and wives and brothers and sisters, and recoiled at the horror of it all.

I did not tell my young companions anything about my own antecedents, thus assuring them of my neutrality and lack of prejudice against any religious or political faction. I was only a writer on a travel assignment for an English publication, knowing a bit of Arabic and something about Islam and the Middle East, which helped communication between us. Salman and Jocelyne proved delightful companions – intelligent, kind and wise beyond their age – and during the week that we travelled together, I learnt much from them. They exemplified the fortitude and resilience of a people who have been through countless calamities in their long history and have pulled through.

The origins of Beirut go back to the Stone Age. Its known history begins with the Phoenicians, who founded the city in the 15th Century BC and called it 'The Bride of the East'. It became important under the Romans; then the Emperor Augustus named it Julia Augusta after his daughter. The first law school was established here and became renowned throughout the Empire as the 'Nurse of Law'. Its teachers helped draw up the code of Roman law on which our European laws are based.

Then came the first of many natural disasters: earthquakes ravaged the city in 529 AD and finished it off in 551. The law school was moved to Sidon in the south, and Beirut lost its prominence. When the Arabs arrived, in 635, they found nothing of significance. The Crusaders occupied it in he 12th and 13th Centuries, and in 1516 the whole country became a province of the Ottoman Empire. Under Fakhroddin al-Maani, the governor between 1585 and 1635, Lebanon achieved a measure of independence, and Beirut began to prosper again. Modelling himself on the Medicis of Florence, Fakhroddin built Italianate palaces, laid out gardens and encouraged commerce and industry. After a while, alarmed by his independence, the Turks lured him to Constantinople and strangled him.

The next upturn in Beirut's fortunes came in the 19th Century, under Emir Beshir. Again the Ottoman sultan intervened; Beshir was captured and taken into exile in Constantinople, where he died ten years later. After World War I, when the Ottoman Empire was splintered and its Middle Eastern dominions divided between Britain and France into 'zones of influence', Lebanon became a French protectorate with Beirut as its capital. Full independence was only achieved after the World War II.

We drove to the centre, then abandoned the car to walk. Before the civil war, Martyrs' Square had been the heart of the city, with gardens and palm trees and outdoor cafés; on one side a covered passage led to the old goldsmiths' souk and the exotic food market beyond. Now the square is a vast empty space, with the pock-marked statue of the martyrs in the middle. The Green Line that divided Beirut into Muslim West and Christian East starts here, along Bechara al-Khouri Street. Blocked with stacks of tyres and burnt-out cars, it was the scene of intense fighting and still bears the scars. In the surrounding streets, bullet-ridden charred skeletons of buildings gape beside new skyscrapers. 'Even during the war people were busy building,' Jocelyne said. She guided me to a side street to show me the model of Solidère: a huge construction project with residential and office buildings, public gardens and recreational spaces, conceived to return the city centre to its former glory. To me, it looked a nightmare of concrete building-cubes stacked by crazy children. That nobody has protested against this monstrosity is explained by the corruption endemic in the Third World. Planning permissions are obtained by greasing the right palms: 60% of Solidère shares belong to ex-ministers and prime ministers. 'People are against this project, but what can they do?' said Jocelyne. I told her that even in the West, where there is no overt bribery, appalling buildings are put up every day, disfiguring beautiful cities, destroying famous sky-lines and prospects, while people watch in despair, unable to do a thing about it. The result of this unbridled greed is an irreparable loss of identity. Viewed from the sea, Beirut was a modern town that could be anywhere in the world: 'Chicago-on-the-Sea' would be a more apposite description than the 'Bride of the East', although it might not be fair on Chicago. Still, what survives from the old Beirut – the majestic sea and colourful variety of people – redeems the city, and in a short time a spell is cast.

Between the square and the port lay Phoenician Beirut, but nothing of it has survived. The war destroyed everything except the American University to the north and the National Museum. There are traces of Roman Beirut nearby – a forum and baths – but not much else. Many of the landmarks cover several layers of history. To the north of the square, the Great

Mosque began life as a temple of Jupiter, then it became the Byzantine Church of St John the Baptist, then it was converted into a mosque by Saladin. To the southwest, the Maronite Cathedral of St George has changed religion several times too – from ancient church to mosque under the Mamelukes, then back again. Both the Great Mosque and the Cathedral were damaged during the war. They were still closed when I was there, though reconstruction is going ahead fast, and by the time this is in print they will probably be in working order. St George is the patron saint of the Lebanon. It is here that he is believed to have slain the dragon, 'to rescue a beautiful princess,' Jocelyne said. (This is confirmed by Gibbon in *Decline and Fall of the Roman Empire*, chapter XXIII.) I told her that St George is also the patron saint of England, so perhaps he slew two dragons? Or has each country its own 'dragon' within and needs a St George to save it by slaying the beast?

Another edifice with a chequered history is the Serail Mosque of Amir Assa, which was first a church – of St Saviour – then a synagogue. Legend says that the Jewish worshippers defaced the image of Christ on the crucifix and that, instead of punishment, this act of desecration provoked a series of miracles whereby the contrite Jews embraced Christianity and turned the place back to a church again. Later, it became a mosque – clearly with the Saviour's approval, since no more retaliatory miracles are recorded.

The Archaeological Museum had just reopened. Its rich contents were hidden away during the war and remained safe. The exhibits come from all over the country and cover Lebanon's six thousand year history. The most striking objects were the sarcophagus of Ahiram, engraved with the earliest alphabetical inscriptions, a mosaic telling the story of Alexander's life and another depicting seven Greek philosophers gathered around the muse Calliope, each with a moral dictum, enjoining virtues such as knowledge and moderation.

Jocelyne wanted me to see Hamra Street, the grandest shopping district in the Middle East before the war. Every famous Western designer had a boutique here; a few of them have reopened lately in newly-rebuilt premises and are slowly picking up business. But walking through the streets is often an obstacle race: entire streets are dug up, others blocked by building machinery, yet others flooded by water works.

It was a relief to reach the residential quarter of East Beirut, which escaped the destruction of the city centre. Some beautiful Ottoman villas here give a hint of the life before chaos. I could see why Beirut was the ideal city for Middle Easterners of my parents' generation: it was supposed to combine the best of East and West – European *chic* and Oriental manners. A friend of my mother's had lived here before World War II, and I remember her describing the magnificent setting, the beautiful houses, the fine style of the life. Now the old houses are run down and forlorn; set amid brooding gardens of ancient trees covered with ivy and scented creepers, they have the nostalgic charm of a vanished era.

One of them is the ravishing Sursock Museum, built at the turn of the 20th Century for Nicholas Ibrahim Sursock, a rich and generous Beirut merchant. It was closing day, but Mr. Saad, the curator, kindly offered to guide me through it. 'There were no architects in those days, just master-builders who followed the specifications of the owner,' he said. 'Sursock lived here with his family and left it to the nation as a museum housing his own collection of art, furniture and carpets.' I remembered hearing about Mrs Sursok, a great beauty, who was said to have been the Kaiser's mistress.

The interior had the discreet elegance of a grand family house, with a fountain at the centre of the Oriental *salon* – 'The water cooled the air, before air-conditioning was invented' –

and all around it magnificent Persian carpets covering the floors, marble seats engraved with Arab proverbs and in the niches delightful *objets d'art*. Next door was the dining-room and the *fumoir*, kept exactly as when the family lived in the house and entertained on a lavish scale. Enormous kitchens and sculleries once filled the basement, employing an army of cooks and servants. Upstairs, the bedrooms have been turned into a large exhibition hall for contemporary art and sculpture. 'The war destroyed the Oriental character of Beirut,' Mr Saad said mournfully. 'The great families were not commercial people, and they have lost everything.'

The Lebanese created their own distinctive architecture within the Ottoman tradition – refined, ornate, in tune with the country's unique setting. But, as elsewhere in the Islamic world, the authentic style has been replaced by ersatz modernism, unsuited to the climate and the way of life. Among the few surviving examples is Lady Cochrane's villa nearby. Even here the civil war has left its marks – bullet wounds on the pilasters and stone walls. Lady Cochrane was away, but the housekeeper was welcoming and showed me around. The house had the faded elegance of a palace long abandoned by its prince. Large rooms divided by slim columns, high ceilings, decorative wrought-iron, ornate plaster and wood carvings, glass and crystal reflecting the silky carpets created a self-contained and gentle world. The villa seemed in need of renovation: 'A great deal of money is needed to keep these old houses in good repair, which the old owners no longer have,' said Mr Saad.

We walked on to the American University, one of the most famous in the Middle East, which survived the war, and today is as lively as ever. It stands on a hill amid well-tended sub-tropical gardens and parks, with a magical view over the sea. It is a favourite spot for the young to roam and picnic.

On our way back to my hotel on the Corniche, we saw the Pigeon Rock, a pair of huge rocks hollowed out by water which can be reached by boat or swimming, for a magnificent view over the city and the coast.

Lebanon is half the size of Wales, only 150 miles long and thirty miles wide. I imagine her as an odalisque reclining between the Mediterranean and the mountains, gazing into infinity. Behind her the Lebanon and the Anti-Lebanon ranges rise to eight thousand feet and are dotted with villages right up to the watersheds. Between the mountains hangs the green Bekaa Valley. The names of the ancient ports along the coast resound with history – Tripoli, Byblos, Sidon, Tyre, with Beirut the largest, a pearl in the centre. These ports were the destination of Eastern caravans at the end of the Silk Road. Here they exchanged their cargoes of spices and textiles for bags of gold.

'The Land of Milk and Honey', the birthplace of the Semitic goddess Astarte (whose Hellenic incarnation was Aphrodite) and of her lover Tammuz/Adonis, Lebanon has always been an object of desire. The Egyptians, the Persians, the Romans, the Ottomans and finally the French, all fell in love with her and stole her away. But the Lebanese have inherited their love of travel and trading talent from their Phoenician ancestors, thought to be the Old Testament's Canaanites, who built ships and navigated by the stars. They took cedar wood to the Pharaohs in Egypt and exchanged it for pink granite from Aswan. They extracted the purple dye from shellfish and sold it abroad. They established ports of call along the Mediterranean and African coasts and became very rich.

In spite of its small size, Lebanon is replete with history and myth. You can spend years exploring the vestiges of the past or

94

a few days visiting the famous sites. I was there in November, a perfect time for exploration: moderate temperature, the countryside ablaze with autumnal colours, the orchards bright with ripe persimmons and apples and plums – but no snow yet for skiers, though the sea was by now too cool for any but the most hardy swimmer.

Since no distance is longer than sixty miles from Beirut, I decided to base myself there for the whole trip. So every morning I set off early with Salman and Jocelyne and returned in the evening, sometimes to dine with friends, who kindly invited me on the basis of an introduction.

The first stop on our way north to Byblos and Tripoli was Nahr-al-Kalb – the Dog River – nine miles from Beirut. So built up is the coast that it seemed we never left the town, just followed the blue shoreline through dense traffic until the mountains rose closer on our right.

Here beside the rushing waters, successive conquerors have carved steles on the steep rocky slopes to mark their passage, much as children scratch their names on stones and trees for memory's sake. From Ramses II's hieroglyphics to 20th Century French and English inscriptions, these memorials punctuate the region's history. The Greeks called the river Lykos – wolf. Legend has it that there once stood on this spot the huge statue of a dog which protected the country from invaders, howling to alert the population whenever their ships approached the coast. The howl may have been the sound of the wind blowing through the narrow mountain corridors and resounding inside this hollowed-out space. Some believe that it was the jackal-dog Anubis, protector of the dead, who accompanied human souls to the next world and helped Isis to find her lost lover Osiris in Lebanon. At any rate, the place owes its sacred reputation to the clear river that flows down from the mountains to disappear mysteriously underground and re-emerge to supply Beirut and its neighbourhood with water.

The oldest inscription on the right bank of the river is in cuneiform. It records the vicissitudes of Nebuchadnezzar in Lebanon and Mesopotamia in 6th Century BC. Seventeen in all, in eight languages, these steles' inscriptions are not numbered chronologically; they leapfrog over the centuries marking salient events. No II is a Latin one commemorating the Emperor Caracalla (211-217 AD), while No III is in Arabic and recalls the Mameluke Sultan Barquq in the 14th Century; No VI speaks of an Assyrian king and No IX of the Allies capture of Damascus and Aleppo from the Ottomans after World War I. Some of the inscriptions have been effaced and replaced by later ones: Napoleon III (*Napoléon le petit*, as Victor Hugo called him) obliterated an Egyptian declaration to commemorate his own expedition in 1860 – an expedition led by Général Beaufort to put a stop to Muslim and Druze persecution of the Maronite Christians.

As we drove off, a tiny kitten under a wild fig tree in a cleft of rock caught my eyes. It was miaowing pathetically, and we stopped to rescue it. It had shiny grey thistledown hair and green eyes, looked beseechingly at Jocelyne as she picked it up and tried to dig its claws into her jumper. Where had it come from? We looked around – nothing but rocks and bushes, no sign of kith or kin, yet it did not look older than a week or two. We stood by the road as cars sped past, holding the kitten up. A van stopped, with four young passengers – two men stretched on the open top looking bored, a couple inside. The girl asked how much we wanted for our kitten, and when I said she could have it free, she put out her hand through the window and grabbed it as the car screeched into gear and sped away, hooting cheerfully.

Turning back, I saw a monk emerge from a black hole on the

mountainside, so lean he seemed to be floating. His habit was girdled with rope, and he had a gaunt, rather beautiful face and fine features, with dark burning eyes, lit by a gentle expression. He told me that he had found the opening to this little cave hidden behind a huge stone and that he had gradually cleared it out and made it into a chapel. Would I like to see? – An underground passage opened out into a small candlelit rock-chamber. An oil lamp hung from the ceiling above a small altar made of a table covered with white cloth; a crucifix hung on the rock-face, a statuette of the Virgin stood on rocks and coloured photographs of saints in flimsy frames were stuck in the hollows. There were bunches of wild flowers in jam jars and clusters of dry corn and grass. 'This was a secret passage to the Monastery of St Joseph on the mountaintop,' the Friar told me. 'The Turks blocked it, leaving only this entrance. One night I dreamed of a dark tunnel, at the end of which was a room full of light. The following day I discovered this place behind brambles and thorns. I have named it the Chapel of St Theresa of Lisieux.'

The friar belonged to the Maronite order of the Brothers of the Cross, and his monastery was miles away in Dora, but he came here often in retreat, sometimes staying for days. I offered to drive him back to his monastery, but he declined. When he was ready to leave, he would walk; and whenever he became tired, some car would stop and give him a lift. 'If you trust in God, He will always help you.'

The friar and Salman were so alike in their piety and innocence, it was hard to imagine they had been on opposite sides in a war. 'It all started with one shot fired by a Christian at a Palestinian bus – but it had been brewing for a long time. We thought it would burn itself out in a few days. Instead, it lasted seventeen years!' Salman shook his head. Yet it is perhaps the purity and prayers of such non-combatants that maintained the spiritual life of the country while the conflagration burnt itself out.

We drove on to Junieh. About ten miles from Beirut, it used to be a small fishing village with covered souks, backed by tree-covered slopes. Then one day they built Beirut's Casino on the edge of the sweeping bay, and development began to change everything. When Beirut became an inferno of civil war, the Beirutis used to get away to Junieh for a change, and hotels, restaurants and nightclubs quickly sprang up. 'We Lebanese love life, and nothing stops us enjoying it,' Jocelyne said. Today the souks are much smaller and done up; the vaulted ceilings have gone, and stalls are filled with knickknacks and frippery, while the little town has grown into a smart suburb and play-ground for the rich. The old fishermen have gone; the Casino, closed during the troubles, has re-opened.

I remembered Junieh as a cluster of russet-coloured roofs and green slopes. Now the trees have been cut down to make room for building, and the town is permanently choked with traffic. 'Before, this was one of the oldest part of the world; now everything is modern,' lamented Salman. 'But people in Casino not care – their eyes fixed on money, they not see the beauty of sunset on the sea.' It is only at night that Junieh recaptures something of its old charm, when it glitters with thousands of lights reflected in the still water.

A funicular built in 1904 took us thousands of feet in an almost vertical ascent to Harissa, on the top of the mountain. The new Cathedral of St Paul, built in the shape of a Phoenician ship, can take very large congregations. On the edge of the cliff stands an immense statue of the Virgin of Lebanon. She faces the sea with her arms outstretched in welcome and blessing. The view spreads in a blue sweep of bay, from Beirut on one side to Byblos far away on the other.

'Young people make the steep ascent on foot as a pilgrimage,' Jocelyne said. 'They say that during the war the Virgin would turn her gaze and cry with real tears. Can you believe that?' 'In a way, yes,' I said; 'I mean, the statue can't cry; it is made of stone and follows the laws of Nature. But the Virgin belongs to a transcendental order, and I can envisage her crying often at the cruelty and misery of human beings.'

Fringed with eucalyptus and palm, the road carried on through orchards and orange groves and banana plantations. All the villages are steeped in history. Jocelyne pointed up to Tabarja Bay, whence St Peter is said to have embarked for Rome. Further on was Amshit, where Ernest Renan and his sister lived for years while he wrote his *Vie de Jésus* – she died and was buried there. Finally, we reached Byblos and plunged into the mediaeval town.

Byblos/Jebail, is one of the oldest human settlements in the world. It goes back seven thousand years. In Pharaonic times its inhabitants established strong trading relations with Egypt, exporting cedar and pine from their mountains to the desert kingdom. In return the Egyptians sold them papyrus, which they exported to the rest of the Mediterranean. The Greeks called the scrolls of papyrus *byblia* – books – which gave the word Bible, The Book, to many languages. The association with Egypt was confirmed in the myth of Isis and Osiris. When the jealous Seth killed Isis' brother Osiris, he put his body in a coffin and threw it in the Nile. Eventually it reached the shore of Byblos, where a beautiful young tamarisk gathered it up and hid it in its trunk. Later, the tree was cut down and made into a column to uphold the roof of the king's palace. Hearing of this, Isis, Osiris's wife as well as sister, went to Byblos and, sitting by the well in the palace, wept disconsolately. The Queen took pity on her and, upon hearing her story, ordered the column to be taken down and the coffin released. Isis returned with it to Egypt, where she brought her beloved Osiris back to life. In time, this tale of resurrection through the power of love metamorphosed into the Greek myth of Aphrodite and Adonis, Lebanon's central myth.

The most spectacular vestige of the Pharaonic period is the splendid fifty foot long solar boat built by Cheops (2549-2526 BC), now in the Museum of the Great Pyramid in Egypt. After the defeat of Ramses II (1279-1213 BC) arrived the 'Sea People' – the Phoenicians, that is – who took over the whole coast and opened trading stations everywhere. Greek, Persian and Roman invaders took the town in turn, the last reviving its fortunes. They built an amphitheatre and colonnades, and the Byzantines added their churches. After the Arab conquest, Byblos sank into gradual decline and became a fishing village strewn with clues to its lost splendour. It was the Crusaders who brought it back to life, built a castle, spread the town and surrounded it with a wall, of which parts are still standing.

We walked through the charming old town, with its stepped lanes and weathered stone walls overflowing with bougain-villaea, hibiscus, laurels and evergreens. In the small bazaar we called on a friend of Jocelyne's, Pierre, at his fossil shop. He has a fossil site in the mountains and offered to show me how they are quarried, then carefully cut open to reveal the anatomies of unfamiliar fish. We made a tentative date for another day and moved on to ancient sites, beginning with the castle.

'It's the first the Crusaders built in Lebanon,' Jocelyne told me. It is surrounded by a deep moat. A superb view from its keep includes the whole town, with its mediaeval heart, its modern overflow and above all its ruins. I wandered among the ramparts, temples, colonnades and tombs, which go back four thousand years. Little remains of a great temple of the goddess Baal-lat – this is the feminine form of Baal – except a few columns and the pool of Astarte/Aphrodite. The Obelisk Temple has lasted better. It is called this because of some thirty obelisks, offerings to the gods, which have survived thanks to the layers of sand and soil that embedded them. It was dedicated to Sheref, an Egyptian sun-goddess who was adopted by Byblos: she was the equivalent of their own goddess Anat, who became the goddess of storm and war.

The town's cemetery contains a group of vertical tombs – shafts dug deep into the rocks – which were probably a measure against grave-robbers. ('Beware! Thy death lies below!') Undeterred, the thieves left only a few objects. The most important is the sarcophagus of King Ahiram, a contemporary of Ramses II, which, as I've mentioned, is now in the Archaeological Museum in Beirut. It bears early alphabetical inscriptions as well as a picture of the king on his throne holding a lotus flower and flanked by a sphinx on either side.

On our way back towards Beirut, we stopped at the Byzantine Church of St John the Baptist. Built in 1115, it has a spacious vaulted nave and carved arches, and some of the columns have been transferred from older buildings. Its cool garden of limes and flowering trees and stone paths had been freshly watered. One loses the sense of time in such ancient places; only the changing aspect of the sea reminded me that it was time to move on.

We reached our final destination in mid-afternoon. Tripoli, which is Lebanon's second largest city, is only 53 miles from Beirut; yet it seemed a different world. Here was a buoyant Levantine port, with a teeming mediaeval town, a thriving Oriental bazaar and mosques, madrassahs and hammams. Hawkers, street-vendors, laden donkeys and cycle-carts wove their way through throngs of exotically attired crowds from all over the Levant. In the distant past, Tripoli consisted of three distinct towns, hence its triple-town Greek name. An earth-quake in 543 AD changed the shape of the port, and a part of the town was swallowed by the sea, which left the city divided into two: al-Mina, the sea harbour, and al-Medina, the actual town. Until recently, two miles of orchards and gardens separated the two parts, but urban expansion has fused them into one huge sprawl of unremitting plainness, only saved on the waterfront by the grandeur of the harbour, its array of ships, its vast horizon and soft breezes that seem to promise release.

Al-Mina was the original Phoenician city, and its history goes back to the 8th Century BC. One of the liveliest Mediterranean ports, it flourished under successive conquerors: the Persians, Romans, Byzantines and Ottomans. Today the 15th Century Tower of Lions is the only interesting relic. It is a fine example of Islamic fortification, with granite columns and the lion of its name in bas-relief. Al-Mina is now the residential quarter, with prosperous blocks, tree-lined avenues and flourishing orange groves. In contrast, the Medina – built by the Mamelukes and Ottomans between the 13th and the 19th Centuries, on the banks of Abu-Ali/Qadisha river which flows from the cedars that grow on the upper levels of the mountains – is the real city. It throbs with life, seething with variegated crowds. The river had sunk to a brownish débris-choked trickle, but Salman assured me that autumn rains and spring floods would wash it clean and bring freshness and fertility to the town and the country around it.

Its banks were lined with trestle-tables of merchandise, anything from farm produce to bales of cloth, and, going down a few steps, we dived into the souks. Tripoli is a devout Sunni city, and I was advised to put on a scarf over my head if I wished to enter the mosques. The maze of vaulted and cobbled lanes is one of the oldest bazaars in the Middle East, going back to the time of the Crusades. Here and there one spots a wrought-iron fanlight, a small square with a fountain, an awning of bright cloths, a mosque or a caravanserai. You can feel your way through by the sounds; the din of brassworkers hammering the inlay into ornaments; the hush of the goldsmiths' souk, its microscopic shops glittering with bangles and filigree; the whirring of old sewing machines in the Khan al-Khayyatin – the 14th Century tailors' quarter, where needle-men are sewing caftans for women and the baggy trousers called shalwars for men, while young apprentices iron them and fold them away. In the Khan al-Sabun – the soapmakers', which was once a 16th Century caravanserai – young boys were decorating square cakes of soap with stylised flowers and fruit. Nearby, drafts of steam issued from the Izzeddin hammam, which was built in 1295; it is the oldest in the city, and still functions. The attendant invited me to peep inside: lit with beaded chandeliers from Damascus, the entrance was carpeted, with shallow flights of sitting ledges. Inside, steam dimmed the air, and men who were naked except for their loincloths, sprawled on marble floors beside steaming basins.

We halted at a mosque where the afternoon prayer had just ended, and the Imam and congregation were coming out. In the middle of the courtyard was the wide basin for ablutions, and above it a verse from the Koran was engraved on the canopy. I managed to read it, but did not quite get what it meant, so I asked one young man. He looked baffled, as if he had never noticed it, much less given it a thought. He smiled, shook his head and asked several of his companions; presently a crowd gathered, each asking the question no one could answer. Yet it was in Arabic, and if anyone could fathom the Word of God surely it would be someone who spoke the same language? At last the Imam intervened: 'It means, "Whosoever glorifies God's commandments / Will have his heart purified."' The poetry and music of the Koranic Verses sometimes make them seem obscure. Few care to probe, believing that reciting the words is sufficient to purify the mind and the soul.

By the time I reached the Great Mosque, the afternoon congregation had dispersed, but here and there lone men were praying in the courtyard and in the prayer chamber. It is the direct dialogue with God and the prostration before Him that makes the sight of a Muslim at prayer so moving. It reminded me of Antoine de St Exupéry, who said that it was seeing a man praying alone in the middle of the vast indifferent wilderness in Algeria, his horse tethered to a stone nearby, that gave him back his own Christian faith. Perhaps St Teresa of Avila was influenced by Spain's Islamic heritage when she decreed, *'No hay menester terceros'* – no need for third-person intermediaries between man and his God. You would have thought that this would have insured Muslims against self-appointed religious demagogues. It has not been the case, alas, as the upsurge of so-called 'fundamentalism' has proven.

The Great Mosque, the oldest in the city, was built at the end of 12th Century by the Mameluke Sultan Qalqun on the remains of the earlier Cathedral of St Mary of the Tower; the rectangular minaret is the old cathedral belfry. This and the lovely north door are the only things of interest, but the whole place, with deep porticoes all round the central courtyard, is impressive. By contrast the beautiful 14th Century Tailan Mosque, with its green domes and columns of Aswan granite, Corinthian marble capitals and grand portal splendidly decorated with Syrian ablaq is worth exploring. (It was built over an earlier Carmelite church.) I lingered before the fine calligraphy of the inscriptions, the decorative wood carvings and floral patterns of the wooden gallery for women, the grand prayer chamber, until Salman reminded me of the time.

We walked quickly along the ramparts to the Crusaders' Castle of St Gilles. Perched high above the city, it was built in about 1100, by Count Raymond of Toulouse, leader of the First Crusade. After a long siege, the Crusaders defeated the Muslim army in 1109. In the massacre and looting that followed, the city's library, the finest in the Islamic world, was burnt to ashes. Its fortunes revived under the Mamelukes, and Tripoli became famous throughout the Muslim world as a seat of learning – particularly for medicine, philosophy, astronomy and mathematics. At its height, the silk-weaving industry here harboured four thousand looms. Today the castle bears the imprint of the Crusaders, the Mamelukes and the Ottomans, who owned it in succession. In its last phase, it was turned into a prison. The maze of halls, banqueting rooms, passages, staircases and stables for hundreds of horses are nearly all open to the sky, but it isn't hard to imagine the life of the inhabitants when it was in its prime, their suffering during the long sieges and appalling massacres. When I reached the ramparts, the magnificent view chased away these gruesome images. It takes in the whole city: the red tiled roofs of the mediaeval town, with its domes and minarets, the tall modern buildings of al-Mina, the crowded port and blue infinity.

There were a number of arrangements for the evening in Beirut, and we drove back vowing not to be deflected. Below the road, the coves, bays and inlets offered snug shelter for bathers. Once open to the public, they are now claimed by developers with their cabins and huts and pools. We stopped above Batroun Beach to gaze down. Steps cut into the cliffside corkscrewed hundreds of feet down to a small chapel of the Blessed Virgin scooped out of the rock, with a minute altar and a forest of candles. It could only hold a few worshippers at a time, and a little party of pilgrims was assembled there in quiet piety.

The sun had turned into a disc of liquid gold, spreading a glistening trail on the water, while a nearly full moon hung between two ridges at the other end of the sky. Then, suddenly, the water was dark and horizon empty: the sun had dropped into the sea, and we had lost the moon turning a bend.

Stuck in traffic jams around Junieh and Beirut, I made frantic calls with Jocelyne's mobile telephone to my next appointment – at The Artisan, a shop opposite my hotel on the Corniche. They were closing at 6.30, but could they wait a bit longer until I arrived? The shop belongs to Nadia al-Khouri, and I had an introduction to her. Petite, with blond curls framing a sun-tanned face and bright humorous eyes, she is one of Lebanon's best designers. After the civil war, she collected craftsmen and seamstresses from all over the Arab world and set them to work – embroiderers from Damascus, coppersmiths and mirror-workers from Iraq, glassblowers from Jordan and inlay experts from Lebanon. The shop is full of exquisite objects and beautiful clothes designed by Nadia and made with time-honoured stuffs. I fell for a claret-coloured velvet dress, embroidered with little pearls and fine gold thread, fit for a princess in a Persian fairy tale. I could not afford it, and she insisted that I take it as a present. Naturally I refused, but I had the pleasure of 'selling' it to a woman from the Persian Gulf by putting it on and parading as if on a catwalk. 'I will have it for my daughter,' she said. It fills me with delight to think of this young girl I have never seen cutting a dash in it.

I had another introduction, this time to Amal, an editor and journalist, who took me to L'Olivier, a restaurant in the residential district of Ashrafieh, for dinner *à deux*. We sat in the little moonlit garden among citrus and olive trees, with a tall palm standing on the corner. Inside, a trio of young musicians and a singer were playing lutes and singing songs of love and forlorn passion. Strains of threnody reached us through the open windows. Amal ordered an array of Lebanese dishes – okra, aubergine, chicken – one more delicious than the other. She hardly touched any herself while I eagerly tried everything; instead, she asked for a nargileh and told me all about her work as the water gurgled in the glass vessel and the aroma of sweet tobacco coiled into the night air.

After the civil war, she had started a legal supplement to one of the country's most popular daily papers: 'to initiate people to their rights; to tell them that they are entitled to the rule of law, as the Constitution provides. Women, in particular, have no inkling about these things.' Recently, the paper's editor had decided to suspend the supplement: 'ostensibly for financial reasons; but, in reality, the powers-that-be have put pressure on him. They don't want people to know what is due to them. They want them to stay ignorant and helpless so that they can be frightened into submission and manipulated.' A sequence of tales about political incompetence and corruption followed, all the banes of the Middle East – rigged elections in which 'dead people vote' and 'voting urns walk', while real voters are intimidated. Caught between the Scylla and Charybdis of Syria and Israel, Lebanon is forced to compromise, and the politicians joyfully fish in the troubled waters. I remembered the wife of a Lebanese minister in a jewellery shop in Damascus choosing the most lustrous and expensive pearls. I guessed where the money had come from. Amal's family of bankers have no need to toe the line, hence her wish to initiate people, regardless of the cost to herself. She and her sister started work at eighteen, to be independent, while her brothers joined the family business. Amal was planning to publish her legal supplement herself, in spite of the distribution problems.

It occurred to me that it is the women in the Middle East who have the strength of character and the courage to bring change about. 'The men are there for the ride,' a local journalist once told me. To me, Amal's intelligent idealism and determination was typical of countless educated Middle Easterners whose ideas and energies are blocked by 'the system', as they call it. A new President had recently been 'elected' who was 'clean'; perhaps things would improve? *'Inshallah!'* she said, evidently doubtful. Amal and I became firm friends, as one often does in the Levant after only one meeting.

So different was the road running south out of Beirut from the one to the north that one might have been in a different country. The outskirts of the city were dusty, overcrowded and run down, with the scars of fighting still raw. The road went through an endless shanty town and was lined with hills of old motor tyres and makeshift shops of spare parts; rickety booths were hitched up among rubble and rocks, loaded with fly-blown slabs of meat, fish and bundles of herbs and vegetables. 'All this part is frequented by refugees and migrant workers from Syria,' said Jocelyne. Thousands have come to Lebanon in search of work, undercutting Lebanese workers by taking much lower wages. Salman told me that he had started his working life as a house-painter but soon had given up, 'because Syrians happy to work for nothing – anything better for them than in home.' So he left to become a driver, which earned a little more. Most of the migrant workers come without their families and stay in crowded quarters and go home just over the mountains when they can.

The south is also more politically active. Photographs of General Lahud, the 'clean' President, Syria's President Assad and religious leaders and martyrs of Hezbollah lined the road – all plastered on crumbling walls and charred houses. Only the aquamarine of the sea relieved the dusty clutter of the slums.

There were Lebanese and Syrian checkpoints, but most of them just waved the cars on. 'The Israeli Army occupies a ten mile zone in the south, which gives the Syrians an excuse to be here,' said Jocelyne bitterly. It seemed that the Lebanese resented their two 'good neighbours' equally and wanted to be rid of them both: 'It is our country; we can deal with it ourselves.' We passed a banana plantation and olive and orange groves and drove through the crowded villages of Damour and Nebi Yunes, the latter named after Prophet Jonah, who is said to have been vomited up here by the whale. Muslims believe that the sides of the whale became transparent, allowing Jonah to spend his time marvelling at the flora and fauna of the deep. I remembered the glass-bottomed boats I had taken in the Caribbean; one could see countless sea creatures and tropical fish as if in a vast aquarium. How thoughtful of the Almighty to have saved Jonah from boredom!

Presently, the Sea Castle rose from the sea on the horizon; we had reached Saida, which is the biblical Sidon. It was past noon, and the loudspeakers of the minarets filled the air with calls to prayer. The seafront was lined with shops, the stalls overflowing with fruit and vegetables. A smell of kebabs grilling floated from a gaily-decorated restaurant. There was a shwarma stand, and displays of Lebanese mezes lured us indoors. We found a table at the back and ordered, while Jocelyne talked about the south. She was saying that the presence of thousands of Palestinian refugees in their camps, the proximity of the Israeli and Syrian armies and uncertainty about the future were among the chief reasons for the palpable poverty and squalor.

It was not always thus. In ancient times, Sidon was the most prosperous city of the coast. 'The first born of Canaan', it was built by the Phoenicians on a sliver of land with a small off-shore island – now entirely covered by the castle. They created a harbour and planted orchards, and a town grew up on the hillsides. From here, they sailed the seas. They were the first sailors to round the Cape of Good Hope, according to Herodotus. In the *Iliad*, Homer refers to richly embroidered robes wrought by Sidonian women and to a Sidonian silver bowl given as prize at the funeral games of Patroclus.

The Sidon we see today is a mediaeval city, and its show-piece is the Crusaders' castle. It was built in 1228 during the Sixth Crusade, after the city and the original castle had changed hands several times in the previous century; Baldwin of Flanders, King of Jerusalem, was followed by Saladin, King Louis IX of France, the Knights Templar and finally the Mamelukes. We went in through the gate and a vaulted hall and made our way into a dark labyrinth of rooms and stairways strewn with columns and capitals, headless lions and fragments of cannon. From the top of the tower, we could look down on the old town with its elongated minarets and shining domes. The sun-bleached sea was empty and still, and in the noon haze one could imagine the ghosts of Phoenician fleets putting to sea, bound for Arabia and Africa.

The old Arab souks were closed for Friday – Muslim Sabbath – but Jocelyne told me that, having escaped renovation, they were the most picturesque of all. We walked through the souks' empty corkscrew of lanes, then on to the Khan Franji, the Caravanserai of the Franks, built for French silk merchants in the 16th Century by Fakhroddin, the semi-autonomous ruler of Lebanon under the Turks. The khan is built round a courtyard, two floors high, surrounded by arcades and decorated with fine black-and-white ablaq. Further along was the Great Mosque, which was empty. It stands on the remains of a basilica of the Knights Hospitaller of the Order of St John. The midday congregation having dispersed, only a few worshippers lingered in the whitewashed and musky nave.

Back on the waterfront, the eywan of the little mosque was

packed with young men sitting cross-legged and listening to the mullah's Friday sermon. 'He is ranting. Words of anger and hatred, designed to fan discord,' Jocelyne said. 'It is fitna [mischief-making]', a grave sin in all religions.

I associated Sidon with the story of Lady Hester Stanhope, the 19th Century English traveller who spent the last twenty years of her life in Joun, a village on the hills above the town. As the niece of Prime Minister William Pitt and his social hostess at Downing Street, Hester had lived at the heart of England's political and social whirlwind. At his death in 1806, the bright lights went out of her life, and, three years later, when her brother and her fiancé were both killed in the war against Napoleon, it became unbearably isolated and dull. The solution was to leave for the Orient. 'There is a longing for the East, very commonly felt by proud-hearted people, when goaded by sorrow,' wrote A. W. Kinglake, who described his 1836 visit to her in *Eothen*. She lived in Damascus and Palmyra in magnificent style, took Arab lovers, meddled in local politics and became famous all through the Middle East. Then, suddenly, she left it all. She bought a monastery at Joun, overlooking the sea. It stood in a garden of roses, among olive groves. She dressed in a huge turban and flowing robes like an Oriental prophetess, became absorbed in magic and astrology, communed with the dead and thought of herself as a seer. The natives thought her mad but humoured her respectfully, and visitors from Europe were impressed by her commanding presence and charmed by her conversation. 'She has features which years cannot alter,' Lamartine wrote. 'I found that no chord was wanting in her high and strong intellect, and that every key that was touched gave out a just, full, and powerful note.' She died there alone in 1839 and was buried in an olive grove close to her house. The climb to her home is a pilgrimage to the shrine of a deeply romantic figure, at the head of a line of great English women travellers who sought in the East an adventure and romance they had lost in their own society.

The road to Tyre, 27 miles south of Sidon, was bordered with citrus groves heavy with fruit. Long transparent cylinders covered the ground like caterpillars – greenhouses for growing vegetables and herbs – and the hills jutted out in granite outcrops like giant mushrooms. Fishermen sat on rocky headlands patiently waiting for a bite. A mile or so from Sidon a huge statue of the Virgin appeared on a mountaintop. She is Our Lady of Mantara, and we made a detour to see the grotto Church of Awaiting. The entrance through three arches led to a spacious cave. On the altar stood an icon of the Virgin-and-Child, her silver crown glittering in candlelight. Long before Christianity, this cave was a sanctuary dedicated to Astarte/Aphrodite; the Christians turned it into a chapel, and in 336 the Empress Helena presented it with the icon of Virgin-and-Child. Hidden by villagers during the persecution of Christians, it was lost, eventually forgotten and survived only as a legend. Then one day during the reign of Fakhroddin, a shepherd boy stumbled in and found the icon shining in the dark. Here the Virgin had waited for her resurrected Son, and He came to see her on His way from Sidon to Galilee (*Mark*, vii, 24).

Twenty-five miles beyond Sidon, we reached Tyre, the southern end of our journey, in the late afternoon. It was hard to believe that this neglected, war-shattered old town, with its haphazard, packed high-rise buildings and its derelict houses, had been the most magnificent port city of this coast for thousands of years. It was called the 'Queen of the Sea' or 'Queen of the South'. Herodotus traced her beginnings to 2730 BC, the dawn of the Phoenician era, but her golden age was in the 11th Century BC during the reign of King Hiram I, a contemporary of King Solomon, when she was described as 'merchant of the people for many isles... Thy borders are in the midst of the seas, thy builders have perfected thy beauty. They have made all thy ship boards of fir trees of Senir: they have taken cedars from Lebanon to make masts for thee. Of the oaks of Bashan have they made thine oars; the company of the Ashurites have made thy benches of ivory, brought out of the isles of Chittim...' (*Ezekiel*, xxvii, 3-6.)

Hiram sent cedar wood from Byblos to Solomon to build the Temple in Jerusalem and a palace worthy of the Queen of Sheba. It was here that the Tyrians dived to fetch the precious purple dye, extracted from the shell of the murex, for the robes of kings and the wide stripes around senators' togas. 'One day,' Jocelyne told me, 'Queen Astarte and her husband King Meqart were walking on the beach with their dog. She noticed that its tongue turned red after eating a shellfish. That was how the dye first came to notice.' In a later version, Astarte turns into Queen Elissa, sister to King Pygmalion. In 814 BC she led a party of disaffected noblemen against her brother. The revolt failed, but she seized the fleet that lay at anchor, loaded with treasure, and sailed to North Africa and founded Carthage. The Greeks called Elissa Dido, or the Beloved, and her doomed love for Aeneas has captured the imagination of poets and composers ever since, despite eight centuries of chronological discrepancy between Aeneas's flight from Troy and the reign of Dido. But what are a few centuries for the imagination, which blends history and myth in response to a deeper human need?

The Phoenicians built Tyre on two offshore islands, each of them with a wide harbour. King Hiram joined them to the mainland; the new city spread and trade flourished; it became a centre of cloth-weaving trade, while its merchant fleet sailed through the Pillars of Hercules and returned from Africa loaded deep with gold, myrrh, ivory and monkeys. When Alexander halted here on his march to Persia, Tyre was the only city to resist him. He spent seven months building a causeway eight hundred yards long and seventy yards wide. He assaulted and won the city, enslaved the women and slaughtered the men. Yet Tyre rose again and prospered and was successively ruled by the customary procession of Greeks, Romans and Byzantines, until the arrival of the Arabs in 633 AD. It changed hands many times during the Crusades, until the Crusaders finally left it in 1291.

The causeway is now the heart of the town, bristling with unprepossessing high-rises and lesser buildings. Its main attraction is a mass of Roman ruins, the 2nd Century city, considerably restored to reveal the layout of its houses and baths, a hippodrome, a forum and large cemetery. The colonnade that runs to the edge of the sea was made of granite from Egypt and marble from Italy with green, brown and white striations, and the place is paved underfoot with geometric mosaics.

Late afternoon is the best time for such ancient haunts, when the light deepens the colours and the sense of mystery. Palm trees cast their long shadows across the stones. A minute frog gleams on a rock; lizards dart away and vanish into crevices; a flight of pigeons circles in the air. A triumphal arch, attributed to Alexander, is in fact Roman, and the hippodrome, where up to twenty thousand came to watch chariot races, has remarkably kept its grandstand and its marble columns intact. Further east, an extensive necropolis is strewn with sarcophagi, which were used again and again by successive people – Phoenicians, Romans and Byzantines, each adding their own decorations. Pagan emblems and pious bric-à-brac peacefully coexist: cupids and crosses, angels and gorgons. The sculptures have been damaged by religious vandals: the Christians sliced the faces off, the Muslims just the noses, and only their wings distinguish the recumbent angels from all the others. Old bones lie beside Coca-Cola bottles and plastic wrappings in some of the sarcophagi.

Back in the mediaeval town, we walked through the streets of the souks, where only a few meat shops were open. The domed ceilings have been replaced with corrugated iron and rags. Some houses are so derelict that their outside stairs seem to hang loose in the air. One of the most inspiring aspects of visiting ancient places like Tyre is to renew one's awareness of human endurance. Wars and natural disasters destroy the entire structure of people's lives, yet still they survive, pick up the pieces and start again. Peace in the Middle East would give places like Tyre hope to recover the past and become whole once more.

Beyond the town were green hills and, beyond them, the Israeli frontier. We sat on the terrace of a café at the edge of town and had tea watching the sun sink into the sea. Then we drove back to Beirut.

I had taken a message to Mr Assem Salam, the doyen of Lebanon's architects, and it had led to an invitation to dinner. He and his Greek-born architect wife Vassa live in a beautiful Ottoman townhouse, which they have most discriminatingly repaired and decorated. A pang of nostalgia gripped my heart as I went in, for it reminded me of our house in Teheran, gone now: the high ceilings, the Persian carpets, the mirrors and glassware, the warm welcome and instant friendship. My new friend Amal was there and a couple of other guests. Vassa gave us a delicious and varied Lebanese feast, and inevitably we talked about politics, the plight of refugees and the Peace Process. How could a tiny country like Lebanon absorb half-a-million newcomers or more? 'It would be as if suddenly 10 million people poured into Britain,' said Mr Hamid. 'Already, with a few thousand refugees from Yugoslavia, the local people in Dover and the other ports are up in protest.' Yet a solution could be found, they believed, if only the politicians were less corrupt and irresponsible and America more even-handed in dealing with regional problems: 'America is now the only superpower; it could establish a *Pax Americana* similar to the Romans' *Pax Romana* and bring peace and prosperity to the world. Instead it behaves irresponsibly, swayed by powerful lobbies.' Meanwhile, everybody muddles through somehow.

'The mountains are the real Lebanon,' a friend had told me, referring to the spoliation of the coast. Not that the mountain villages were spared by the civil war. Some were flattened beyond recognition, and among them was Tarshish, Jocelyne's birthplace: 'One day an empty Christian house was dynamited and the next day a Muslim house was demolished in retaliation, and so it went on until nothing was left. Most of the villagers were working in town, so there was no fighting, just mindless destruction. The village mosque has been repaired now, but the church was beyond saving, and they have built another one further away from the middle. The government gives $1500 to each family to rebuild their house with. It is too little. I wonder if the village will ever come back to life – everybody is settled in town now.'

We took the Sidon route to the south again, but at Damour, about nine miles from Beirut, the road branched left and began to climb the slopes of Mount Lebanon towards the Shouf region. It coiled around the mountains, rising to precipitous heights, through a landscape of woods and valleys. There were cultivated terraced hillsides and rocky wilderness. Patches of misty cloud drifted in the silent valleys below and hovered above the pines and cypresses and poplars that marked their boundaries, clinging to olive branches like silk veils shot with gold. The Shouf is the country of the Druze, whose present leader, Walid Jumblat, is the last in a long line of noblemen whose families have ruled over the region for centuries. A cabinet minister after the end of the civil war, Jumblat is a fervent conservationist who even during the war never stopped planting thousands of trees and protecting the forests and their fauna, Jocelyne told me. For that reason, in spite of old enmities between the Druze and the Christians, he is respected by the different communities. The origins of the Druze are obscure. Some say they came from Arabia and spread over the mountains of Syria and Lebanon; others believe that they are Persians; yet others maintain that they are descendants of the Crusaders, which would explain their pale complexion and often fair hair. Their religion is a blend of Islam, Zoroastrianism, Gnosticism and Christianity, and they have kept their distinctive costumes and customs despite the erosion of modern life.

After a while we reached Deir-al-Qamar – the Monastery of the Moon, so called because excavations revealed a Byzantine stone with the face of the moon carved on it. It is the emblem of our Lady of the Mount, the town's patroness. But the cult of the moon goes back to antiquity, when it represented the Feminine Principle, the Mother Moon harmonising with the Father Sun to create fertility and abundance. It became the symbol of the great goddess Astarte, whose statues were endowed with crescent horns, and in time passed from Astarte to the Virgin; and the symbolism has endured to this day. It inspires fear and reverence in farmers and gardeners, who plant, sow and reap in accordance with the moon's movements. My own sister is named Badri after the moon's radiance, and I remember summers in the country in Persia when farmers worked through the night by the light of her beams, until the goddess faded at dawn.

A pretty, cheerful town, Deir-al-Qamar has much of the charm of the Levant – coral-coloured roofs, weathered stone houses, balconies and verandas full of flowers, everywhere decorative pepper trees with feathery leaves and bunches of little red berries. For fifty years, from 1585 to 1635, Emir Fakhroddin Maani II, Lebanon's national hero, made this mountain town his capital. He spread harmony between he different factions and ruled Lebanon as a country almost independent from the Ottomans. His reign came to an end when they lured him to Constantinople and killed him, but many of the buildings around the town square were put there by him and/or by the Shehab family, who succeeded his dynasty in the 18th Century.

Inspired by the Medicis, Fakhroddin dreamed of turning his mountain capital into a new Florence. He brought over Tuscan architects and gave them free rein; they raised the gathering of original and beautiful buildings which give the town its attractive Italianate air. We walked through sunny paved streets, visiting what remains of a glorious past: the Fakhroddin mosque, and the minaret which repeated earthquakes have gently tilted; the Kharj barracks which housed Fakhroddin's mercenaries; the silk khan, with its arcades and its pool, now magnificently restored and turned into a French cultural centre; the palace of the Shehabs. Some of the old buildings have been converted into private houses, such as a Jesuit monastery. This stands next to the town synagogue, testifying to the tolerance Fakhroddin's reign fostered among his people. Perhaps it did not penetrate deep enough: in 1842 strife broke out again between Druze and Christian; this led to a civil war and the massacre of ten thousand Maronites. Such memories provoke doubt about the present concord prevailing between various groups. Long may it last.

At a fountain near the mosque, women were filling their pitchers with water: 'They say if you drink water of this you go crazy,' Salman said; 'but everybody do it, so everybody crazy to fighting.' He made pugilistic gestures with his clenched fists, laughing. I cupped my hands and quenched my thirst – marvellous. Salman tut-tutted. 'I risk nothing,' I said; 'I'm already mad.'

In the 17th Century when Fakhroddin's family was succeeded by the Shehabs, who ruled for about 150 years, they built their family palace to the west of the square and adorned it with a huge gate studded with jewels. By the end of the 18th Century, a triumvirate of three child princes inherited; they lived in royal mansions, but in a deft coup their cousin Beshir put out their eyes, usurped their position and killed their tutor, Jirjiz Baz. (By a twist of fate, Baz's descendants later bought the Shehab palace, and they own it to this day.) Emir Beshir remained in power for fifty years; ruthless with opponents, he was an able administrator and a generous patron. When his court poet Pierre Karmeh told him that in a dream he had seen a palace of his own, Beshir built him a palace in secret and gave it to him as a present.

Beshir was privately converted to Christianity. This secured him the allegiance of the Maronites and opened his court to foreign missions. His great monument, and the Shouf's showpiece, is Beiteddin, a magnificent palace he built three miles further along the valley, with stunning views over the surrounding countryside. On our way there, we stopped at Moussa Castle, a miniature Crusader citadel built by an expatriate businessman of Syrian origin. It is said that Mr Moussa wanted to win the heart of a woman who had demanded a castle; but according to Jocelyne, this is romantic exaggeration. It is more probable that he was a rich man who enjoyed indulging fantasies about Crusaders and Franks. At any rate, he designed the toy castle himself: it has turrets and ramparts, and every stone on the facade is carved with a different design. There is a museum inside – a sort of Madame Tussaud's of 19th Century Lebanese village life, with wax models engaged in various country tasks – and there is a model of old Jerusalem with camels and goats and people belonging to all three religions that descend from Abraham living together in harmony. 'It is a childish place, but people love it.' – This was quite true: the building was crowded with noisy children and grown-ups. Perhaps the child in everyone responds to Mr Moussa's fantasies of chivalry and triumph.

From afar, for its part, Beiteddin looks like a mirage hovering in the mountain air. Cypresses and poplars mark its confines, and fields and orchards cataract all round it down the valley. A vaulted entrance leads into an immense courtyard surrounded by buildings of *Arabian Nights* splendour. Beshir engaged the best Damascene master-builders and artisans, and they spent thirty years making his dream come true. Handsome porticoes and slim columns encircle the gardens; fountains whisper and crystal streams flow; roomy kitchens, ample stables, splendid reception rooms and hammams of marble – it is a microcosm of the Ideal City, a sort of Lebanese Alhambra. When it was finished, Beshir moved the whole of his administration from Deir-al-Qamar to the new palace.

The palace was divided into three: the Outer House (Dar-al-Baranieh) where guests were welcomed and entertained for three days with no questions asked. It is a museum now, showing a variety of precious items, among them a sword presented to the Emir by Napoleon, a letter from Palmerston and the Shehabs's family tree. The Middle House (Dar-al-Wusta) was the administration; meanwhile, the stables below housed the

Emir's six hundred Arab thoroughbreds. These are a museum now, with a collection of 6th and 7th Century Byzantine mosaics excavated at Nebi Yunes – the village on the coast named after the prophet Jonah. But perhaps the most evocative part of the palace is the exquisitely decorated and sumptuously furnished al-Harem, the private apartment of the Emir and his family. Intricately carved and painted cedarwood ceilings, silk-carpeted floors, elaborate Venetian chandeliers, a hammam with delicate marble columns and basins of alabaster and resplendent mirrors reflecting the rooms at beguiling angles compose a heady and exotic dream. There was an ingenious heating system for the baths, while a scent of orange blossom and jasmine drifted in through the windows. Emerging from the hot chamber, the bathers would loll on silken cushions and smoke their nargilehs and sip cool sherbets, while 'slaves glided about silently… to wipe our hands with gold embroidered napkins'. So wrote the Irish writer Eliot Warburton, who enjoyed the Emir's hospitality. Lamartine too rhapsodised about life at Beiteddin in his *Travels to the East*; he describes the pageantry, the priests and courtiers' black slaves, bristling with gem-encrusted daggers. The poet's portrait hangs in the room where he lodged.

When his favourite first wife died, Beshir sent for three Circassian girls from Constantinople and married the most beautiful one. He surrounded himself with poets and welcomed Western writers, who left enchanted by his lavish hospitality and the grandeur of his court. But once again the Emir's independence and political manoeuvring proved too much for the Ottomans, who deposed him and took him to Constantinople, where he lived in exile until his death in 1851. His widow sold the palace to the Lebanese government, but nearly a century later, in 1947, Beshir's ashes were brought back from Turkey and placed in the tomb of his first wife, Sittes-Shams, in the shade of cypress trees in a garden of roses.

As I wandered from room to room, it was not Lamartine who came to my mind, but another poet who seldom travelled after his one youthful journey to the Indian Ocean. It was something in the décor and mood and ambience of Beiteddin that called Baudelaire to mind and his 'Invitation au voyage':

> *Des meubles luisants,*
> *Polis par les ans,*
> *Décoreraient notre chambre...*
> *Les riches plafonds,*
> *Les miroirs profonds,*
> *La splendeur orientale...*
>
> *Là, tout n'est qu'ordre et beauté,*
> *Luxe, calme et volupté.*

When Beshir married his second wife, he did not wish his three young sons to be too close to her, so he built each of them a small palace nearby. Amin's – the youngest – built on top of a hill above Beiteddin, is now the Mir Amin Hotel. We sat by its pool and ordered a cup of sweet coffee scented with cardamom, lost in gazing over the sweep of the valley and the green slopes beyond. Susanne, a guide and a friend of Jocelyne's joined us, and inevitably again talk turned to politics. 'We are the war generation,' she said. 'While it was going on, it was normality to us, as if it would never end; everyone was involved. Now we are sick to death of politics! We don't trust ideologies or leaders any more; we want work and security to enjoy life. Of course there are still fighters, but most are fed up with conflict.'

Walid Jumblat and his wife Nora live in their own palace, Mokhtara, another magical residence in the Shouf. Their palace was restored by the veteran architect Assem Salam, who was the new friend who had introduced me to them. We stopped at the gate. The gatekeeper asked who I was, and as I was explaining, a young man with a submachine gun appeared and just waved us in. A long drive led us to the house; I rang the bell; Mr Jumblat himself opened the door, and when I introduced myself he called out to his wife, who came and welcomed me in. I had seen Walid Jumblat on television during the civil war, defending his position forcefully, manoeuvring among various factions. Here was a dignified, courteous man welcoming a stranger. I was amazed that no one checked my identity or searched me. For all they knew I could have been a terrorist with a pistol in my pocket. Had the Salams contacted them on my behalf? It turned out that no message had reached them, yet they had opened their door to me in complete trust and welcomed me in. This is a disarming side of the Middle East – you mention the name of a friend, and immediately all doors are opened. Perhaps this spontaneous warmth explains their frequent internecine fights: the sense of betrayal is more acute if one has held nothing back, committed oneself wholly from the start. It is hard to live up to such generosity, let alone reciprocate it, if one belongs to a more reticent tradition where affection and trust are built up gradually over a long period and expectations are within bounds.

Nora Jumblat is tall and slim, with skin like ivory and fine features dominated by lovely eyes; she is in fact spectacularly beautiful. We sat in a small drawing-room over coffee, and she told me about the music festival she organises at Mokhtara every summer, inviting virtuosi from all over the world. It lapsed during the war, but she revived it the moment the fighting ended: 'It took a couple of years to rebuild, but now it's firmly established again.' She seemed keener to tell me about the house and her husband's work than to talk of her own activities: 'The original house was built four hundred years ago, and bits have been added from time to time to enlarge it. Where we are sitting is 150 years old. The old arrangement has been kept up – three buildings round an inner courtyard. We get the water from the mountain called Barouk; it flows to the village and beyond in open channels and drops into the sea at Sidon.' It wells out in front of the house into a limpid fountain under the branches. Looking down, I could drink in the general layout of the place, the walls and balconies, venerable trees and astonishing views. 'My husband has planted hundred and fifty thousand trees – pine, eucalyptus, plane trees and many other. The Barouk Forest, two miles away, has over four hundred cedars said to be over a thousand years old. Everyone talks about the cedars in the north, but there are many more in the forest here, and much larger ones.' The Barouk Forest is a national park now, and the wildlife is protected – there are deer, wolves, wild boars and millions of birds. 'Next time you come we'll make an excursion. It takes two or three hours, and it is wonderful. Do come back.'

We took the mountain road back to Beirut. The sky grew dark and the mountains lost their sharp contours. Below, village lights in the valleys were a string of constellations.

The story of Adonis is Lebanon's essential myth. A myth is a journey of the collective soul, a mirror in which each generation sees its own image reflected. King Arthur in England, for instance, or the hero Rustam in Persia – myths define and sublimate the history of their people. It is fitting that Lebanon with its charm and grace should be the stage of the love story between Beauty and Youth, in the forms of Aphrodite and Adonis. This tale of eternal lovers has been a source of inspiration for poets and bards for thousands of years. Through it, they have expressed their own longings and sorrows.

The origins of the Adonis figure are lost in the mist of antiquity. To the Sumerians he was Tammuz, lover of the Great Earth Mother Ishtar; every year he died, and Ishtar searched for him throughout the land of the dead. In Lebanon, the earliest version of his tale is Phoenician: Astarte, the goddess and patron of Byblos, fell in love with the god Baal; he was killed by a wild boar, leaving her mourning forever. In time Baal underwent several avatars and eventually turned into the beautiful Adonis, whom the Egyptians identified with their own Osiris. We know the story through its Greek and Roman variations: Adonis is born of the incestuous union of King Cinyrus of Byblos and his daughter; upon seeing the child, Aphrodite is so struck by his beauty that she hides him in a chest which she entrusts to Persephone. Dazzled by the infant when she opens the chest, Persephone refuses to return him. In the dispute that ensues between the two goddesses, Zeus inter-venes, decreeing that each should keep him for a third of the year, the remaining third to be at his own disposal. In another version, Adonis is gored and killed by a wild boar while hunting, and so great is Aphrodite's grief that Zeus takes pity on her and allows Adonis to return from the underworld for half the year – thus beginning the eternal cycle of the seasons. Aphrodite was adopted by the Romans, who called her Venus and retold her story in their own fashion. In both Greek and Roman traditions, the goddess is married to the god of war, Ares and Mars respectively, who, jealous of her all-consuming love for Adonis, metamorphoses into a wild boar and gores him to death. Thus the myth places Aphrodite, the goddess of beauty and love, at the centre of creation, for without beauty there would be no love, and without love no reason for being.

The Christians naturally identified the goddess with the Blessed Virgin – the Mater Dolorosa – while the Muslims attached her cult to Zahra, the Prophet's daughter and embodiment of all womanly virtues. Later still, Adonis became St George and the wild boar the dragon he slays, his victory symbolising the triumph of Good over Evil through spiritual chivalry, which is 'fotowa' in Arabic and an important concept in Islamic mysticism.

The Adonis River, locally called Bahr Ibrahim, pours into the sea a mile or so south of Byblos, the 'City of the Goddess', but its source is 25 miles away in the Afqa Grotto, in the heart of the mountains. The Greeks called the place Aphaca, 'the Kiss', which became the Arabic Afqa, or 'source', and it was here that the lovers exchanged their first and last kisses. When Adonis was gored by the wild boar, Aphrodite tried to revive him but failed, and he died in her arms. Ever since, scarlet anemones have grown on the banks of the river where his blood flowed.

Every spring when the river thunders out of the cave and rushes towards the sea, 'it loses its colour and takes on the hue of blood. At its mouth a wide fan of the sea is dyed red, and the people of Byblos know that it is time to go into mourning. They say, at that time, "Adonis is wounded!"' So wrote Lucian of Samosata in 148 AD. Seven days of mourning and lamentation followed: 'He is dead!' the women wailed, beating their breasts, 'Adonis the beautiful is dead!' Then, on the eighth day, the god returned, causing an outburst of joy and celebration: 'He has risen! Adonis has risen!' To this day, mountain villagers commemorate the death and resurrection of Christ by placing 'Adonis Gardens' on their window sills at Christmas and Easter.

On our way towards Afqa, Jocelyne suggested that we should keep our promise to her friend Pierre and meet him at the Shrine of St Sharbel, from where he could guide us to his fossil site. A ship had caught fire a furlong off the bay and was burning furiously when we set off, as if the water itself were ablaze. Clouds of black smoke surrounded the vessel, and a crowd had gathered on the shore, mesmerised by the fireworks. But there was no sign of rescue. Salman said this happened from time to time and that the fires eventually burned themselves out. I marvelled at the nonchalance, but in a country that has seen so many calamities, what's a ship on fire?

Presently, we turned towards the mountains and lost sight of the sea. 'The villages in this part of the country are Christian,' said Jocelyne, which explained the presence of roadside shrines at the sharp bends – a tiny statue of the Virgin in a glass case, a lit candle at her feet, protecting travellers from accidents. Gradually, the hills turned bare, save for some thorn bushes and dwarf evergreens, until we reached the Church of St Sharbel at the summit.

Sharbel was a hermit who lived on this mountain and died in 1898 at the age of seventy. 'After his death people saw light shining on his tomb at night,' Jocelyne recounted, 'and one day a photographer was taking pictures hereabouts and the saint appeared like a ghost in one of his prints. So pilgrims began to come from all over the country, and there were miracles. In 1950, a doctor opened the saint's grave and found his body intact. Not the slightest sign of decay, as though he had just been buried. So they built a church over his tomb and a village, Arraya, grew up around it, and the Pope beatified him in 1954. The saint went on healing the paralysed and incurable and finally, in 1996, he was canonised.'

The crypt of the church was teeming with visitors. Besides the saint's monastic habit, a glass case held an eerie collection of crutches and artificial limbs, belonging to supplicants miraculously healed. Not surprisingly, no recent miracle has been reported. Perhaps in an age that combines disbelief and credulity, lack of religious faith and superstition, even the saints give up.

Pierre met us outside the church, and we drove through the mountains to his fossil mine. It lay among the rocks in a shallow crater. The mountainside was strewn with new houses: 'Summer places for the Beirutis,' Pierre explained. The Lebanese are their old entrepreneurial selves again, and these chalets in the mountains are the fruit of their new confidence and wealth. 'In winter these hills are covered with snow, and people come to ski,' he went on. Pierre himself is a ski champion. Tiny and gentle, he does not look like champion material at first glance, but Jocelyne confirmed his glory.

A twelve year old boy and a middle-aged man were working on the rocks where the fossils were embedded. Pierre asked the man to demonstrate. He picked up a piece of rock, hit it softly on the side with a tool, and the rock opened, revealing a small fossil fish, amazing in its details, a cross between a seahorse and a miniature ray. 'One of the tens of thousands of species that have become extinct,' said Pierre, who has a concession from the government to mine the site. He takes the fossils to his shop in Byblos, where they are mounted and priced according to their marine status.

We dropped Pierre back by the church and wound our way towards Afqa Grotto. The road was empty under an arching sky of flawless blue; only the sun was haloed in autumn haze. Orchards glowed in the valleys; the poplars quivered in a light breeze. I imagined the landscape in the spring, the fruit trees alive with blossom and the air heavy with the scent of orange flowers; and I remembered that Renan pronounced Afqa one of the most beautiful places in the world. At a bend, an old man appeared hunched on a donkey: 'How far to Adonis Grotto?' we asked. 'The time it takes to smoke a cigarette,' he smiled and rode slowly on; and suddenly we were there. Jocelyne pointed to a huge, black, gaping hole in the mountainside, above a tumble of boulders and rocks. A trickle of limpid water emerged and snaked along the stony river bed. Three elderly women had set up a table and some chairs and were picnicking near a graceful stone Roman bridge. Large pipes, carrying water from deep down in the cavern lay along the side of the mountain, and we scrambled over them to peep inside. It was a dark, seemingly bottomless abyss filled with the echo of trickling water, with the mountain rising hundreds of feet overhead. Suddenly a young man emerged, as if from nowhere. But for a shotgun, I would have taken him for the ghost of Adonis. He was lean, handsome and agile, just as the godlike shepherd boy appears in carvings. Was he hunting for game? 'I think he is after bats in the cave,' Jocelyne said. 'If you rub the face of a newborn baby girl with bat's blood, she'll never be hairy and will always have a clear complexion.' He did not want to be photographed, for fear of being harassed by the police. He waved, skipped over the pipes and the stones like a faun and disappeared down the riverbed.

Geologists attribute the blood of Adonis in the soil to the iron ore it contains, but the ancients, who believed that the blood of an innocent god was needed to redeem the earth and make it fertile, may have been closer to the truth. In Persian mythology, as narrated by Firdowsi in *The Book of Kings*, and echoing the story of Phaedra and Hippolytus, it is Siavosh, a young hero wrongly accused by his stepmother and killed, whose blood is the agent of redemption and renewal. The fiery anemones in Persian fields are said to be drops of Siavosh's blood.

It is said that, after the coming of Islam, the Persians adapted this ancient myth to the story of Imam Hossein, the Prophet's grandson, whose martyrdom is mourned by Shias in Persia as well as in Lebanon, where the saint is closer to Adonis than to his Persian counterpart. In the Shia village of Khirbet Afqa, a mile further down the road, the Imam's Passion is commemorated every year with processions and, Salman told me, mourning ceremonies. In its various forms, the myth illustrates the idea that redemption depends on sacrifice, but why it should be so is part of the mystery of Being. One result is the culture of sacrifice among the Shias, and I recalled the processions during the mourning season for Imam Hossein – the chanting, weeping, chest-beating by men in black mourning clothes. How this unconscious deep tendency can be exploited by dictators and demagogues is evident in the events of the recent history of the region.

All around Afqa once stood temples dedicated to Aphrodite and Adonis, but they were destroyed in the 4th Century by the armies of Constantine, at his orders, when St John Chrysostom preached against the cult of the 'licentious goddess'. The granite columns and hewn ashlars of the Temple of Venus bear witness to the importance of her rites. In one carving, Aphrodite is seated with her head bowed in sorrow, one hand raised to her face, as if to hide her tears. Her posture of desolation is said to have inspired early Pietàs. I was reminded of an 18th Century song by an anonymous poet, which I learnt years ago and have sung ever since:

> *Underneath a Cyprus shade the Queen of Love lay mourning;*
> *Casting down the rosy wreaths her heavenly brow adorning,*
> *Drowning fiery sighs with tears,*
> *But yet her heart, but yet her heart*
> *Still burning…*

It occurred to me that the story, in all its variations, focuses on the unassuageable grief of the woman at the loss of love, while the beautiful young shepherd remains strangely passive and evanescent, as he tends to do in Shakespeare's poems.

Perhaps it has ever been thus, and the myth suggests what we know to be true – that for women loss of love is a greater catastrophe than for men and they reach depths of despair men seldom attain.

Nearby, a wild fig had broken out through the rocks. It was festooned with tatters from ill people's clothes; it is an ancient form of prayer for recovery from illness. Wherever a tree defies its habitat and survives on unpropitious soil, it acquires a sacred dimension. I once came across a lone almond tree in the mountains of Persia similarly covered with bits of cloth.

I was glad to find Afqa empty and still, the crickets singing in the bright noonday and the birds rummaging among the ruins, the ghost of the heavenly lovers united in human memory. I could almost hear Adonais's voice as Shelley conceived of it :

> ...in all her music, from the moan
> Of thunder, to the song of night's sweet bird;
> He is a presence to be felt and known
> In darkness and in light, from herb and stone...

By contrast to the haunting solitude of Adonis's grove, the Jeita caves were clamorous with visitors. Four miles from the sea, they are the chief source of the Dog River and Beirut's water supply. Thought the most beautiful in the world, the caves were discovered in 1836 by an American called Mr Thompson, who was out shooting and who reported his discovery to the authorities in Beirut. In 1873 Maxwell and Bliss, two engineers from the Burt Water Company, decided to explore 'Thompson's Grotto' and set off on a raft of inflated goatskins, rowing along a seemingly endless river under the mountain. They put the record of their exploration in a bottle and set it on a stalagmite, where it has remained ever since, decorated now with an opalescent lace of mineral growth. Other explorers followed, going deeper into the heart of the mountain and finding a vast maze of galleries, canals, pools and lakes, filled with amazing stalagmites and stalactites. The opening ceremony in 1969 was a grand international affair, with concerts and fashion shows, and the caves became one of Lebanon's most popular attractions. The composer Stockhausen was among the first to give a concert in the upper gallery, which can seat five hundred. Damaged during the civil war, when they were used as secret ammunition depots, the caves were swiftly repaired and re-opened at the end of it.

Today they are illuminated, and the fast currents of water have been tamed by diversions to allow boats to glide over a smooth surface for half a mile. I climbed a slippery ramp to the upper gallery for a general view and looked giddily down. Born of the mists and the lights, rainbows hung in the air; sounds boomed and echoed; hundreds of feet below, a huge pool glittered. Going down again, I got into a boat; the boatman was impassive like a messenger from the underworld, and so limpid were the glassy depths that the bottom gleamed as we glided in a fantastic world of strange beauty – with marble palaces and cathedrals and forests all deserted and silent. The only sound was the loud drip of water echoing in the empty chambers. A weeping willow, then a camel, and further on a minaret, all turned into marble and alabaster as if by magic. This enchanting phantasmagoria has been brought into being over millions of years by the rain seeping through the limestone, tingeing the opaline accumulation with touches of colour, and sometimes it has a glitter like diamond. Presently the boatman touched the rock-face with his oar, and the boat swivelled round for its return journey.

Once the mountains of Lebanon were covered with cedars. 'Exalted above all trees of the field', their aromatic and sturdy timber was coveted by the Pharaohs and the Old Testament kings for their shipyards and temples. But centuries of over-felling and other woes have left only a few groves standing, of which the most ancient example is one particular group high on Mount Lebanon above Tripoli in the Kadisha Valley (the Valley of the Saints) about 75 miles from Beirut. The grove is one of Lebanon's most cherished treasures, and the majestic tree stamped on her flag is the symbol of her sovereignty.

The road north to Tripoli branched off towards the mountains, climbing and twisting and at times running close to the precipitous Kadisha Gorge. The spiritual heart of Maronite Lebanon, the area has been sheltered from the perils of the coastline. Even the Ottomans left it alone, so long as their tribute was paid. The sect takes its name from St Maron, a hermit who lived in Syria in about 400 AD. After the Council of Constantinople in 681 which condemned their monothelite belief – that Christ has two natures, divine and human, but a single divine Will – the Maronites took refuge from persecution in these mountains. Carving the rocky slopes into terraces, they laid out fields and orchards and built villages on the ledges above the chasm. Travelling in Lebanon in 1831, Lamartine likened the Sacred Valley to 'a vast nave with the sky for ceiling', and so it has remained to this day.

We passed Ehden, with its russet roofs and pretty houses clinging to the mountainside, and stopped on a high ridge above the village of Besharre to gaze at one of the most beautiful views in the whole country. Villages hung from cliffs, steeples rose from pinnacles, and in the far distance Tripoli and the sea shimmered in the haze. 'Without the mist you can see Beirut,' said Salman. A path leads to the river valley and the many chapels and monasteries and hermit's grottoes carved out of the mountains. 'You can see them,' said Jocelyne, 'but it means an entire day along a footpath. In the old days pilgrims walked for twelve days to get here and see the holy places.'

Besharre is famous today for being the birthplace of the mystic poet Kahil Gibran (1883-1931), author of *The Prophet*. His childhood home, a traditional Lebanese stone house, has been kept as it was when he left it at the age of sixteen to spend the rest of his life in America, while in the village the old monastery of St Sergius has become the Gibran Museum, which contains his manuscripts, paintings and photographs.

In winter, the area is a ski resort, with good hotels and restaurants and private chalets, and in summer, a cool refuge from the heat of the cities. But November is a hollow season; the holiday houses are shuttered, and the villages seem deserted. Then, suddenly, there were the cedars, towering hundreds of feet from their valley bowl and spreading a sweeping green canopy. Their enchanted grove was empty and quiet, except for the crunch of the needles underfoot and birds twittering in the branches. Among the Christians, the grove is called the Cedars of the Lord, but for ancient pagans these trees themselves were live and eternal deities. Roaming among them, I really was conscious of a presence. It is often the case in hallowed places. Some of the trees are two thousand years old, but the place seems a haunt of even more ancient wisdom.

A low wall protects part of the grove from goats; it was a present from Queen Victoria. The trunk of one tree is carved with Byron's initials, though it is doubtful that he ever reached these parts; another bears the names of Lamartine and his daughter Julia, who tried to visit the grove but were prevented from reaching it by snow storms. They say that these cedars can 'tell the seasons': at the approach of winter blizzards they 'contract their vast branches like limbs and point them earthward so as to support in the ensuing months the minimum weight of snow. In the spring... they shake off the melting snow... and extend their branches once more,' according one commentator. I can believe it. Some country people in Persia think trees have souls and feel injuries like human beings.

Back on the road a souvenir shop was open, packed with things in cedar wood. A young *pirograveuse* was sitting in the sun decorating the objects with a sort of fire-pencil that engraved wood by singeing the surface. I sat beside her, mesmerised, watching cedar trees and flowers appear on the wood in silhouettes as she plied her singeing tool. She burnt my name on a keyring in ornate letters and gave it to me as souvenir, refusing payment. 'Next time you come.' My house keys still hang on the ring. The name has faded, but I hope I shall never lose it.

I put the Bekaa Valley and Baalbek at the end of my journey on purpose. We avoided the choked coast road and cut through crooked lanes to the Beirut-Damascus highway. It ran through spiky mountains among castellated peaks and rose to a five thousand foot pass. Villages crowned the peaks or huddled in folds; there are rough stone walls and poplars along the climbing terraces. The burnished green of vineyards and fruit trees contrasted with the earth-brown of fields. We stopped at a bend for a glimpse of Tarshish, Jocelyne's village, on a hill far away. The white dome of the recently repaired mosque shone amid ruins like a fallen moon.

Bellow us the Bekaa Valley spread between the two ranges of Lebanon and Anti-Lebanon like a table spread by the gods. Watered by two great rivers, the Litani and the Orontes, it is the widest sweep of agricultural land in the country. Bekaa means 'spots', and it refers to the many-coloured mosaic of cornfields and vineyards that cover the rich red soil. I could imagine the same landscape in spring, when lingering strata of snow glitter on the pink granite rocks and the valleys are strewn with wild tulips and asphodels. In the past, caravans of camels threaded along narrow tracks, the sound of their bells echoing through the hills. Today overflowing lorries lumber on the surfaced highway.

Shatura is well known for its sweet wines and healing waters. It used to be an overnight halt for caravans between the desert and the sea; now it is a pause for tourists. We drove through it to Zahle. Nicknamed 'the Bride of the Bekaa', this town cascades down the mountain to both sides of Bardouni river, and it is famous for its wines and farm produce. The population is mainly Christian, which explains the statues of the Virgin everywhere. When we were there, portraits of Hezbollah martyrs and political leaders hung on walls and lamp posts. 'The Lion will lead you always,' proclaimed the slogan beneath the picture of President Assad of Syria – Assad means lion in Arabic. 'Yeah, he lead you with a stick and in the end he eat you,' Salman spit. 'The Syrians and the Israelis want the Bekaa to feed their populations; all their other arguments are excuses,' Jocelyne added.

The streets above the river are lined with restaurants and cafés and shops. They were packed with swarthy local men smoking hubble-bubble and fidgeting with their beads. We stopped at a crowded place for a cup of Turkish coffee and cakes, to the accompaniment of amplified Arab music. An unmistakable voice came on. It was that of Fairouz, Lebanon's great *diva* – warm, velvety, passionate, heartbreaking in its profound pathos. I asked Salman what the words of her song meant, having just understood 'habibi' – 'darling'. 'All about love – what else matter? She sometime singing patriot song. But that is love also.'

We left town via a road lined with fruit and vegetable stalls set up in the shade of poplars and oaks – mounds of radishes, tomatoes, potatoes, pomegranates, dates and grapes. Jocelyne said that in the nearby village of Karak Nouh, there is a fragment of a Roman aqueduct which is supposed to be Noah's tomb. (Nouh is Arabic for Noah.) 'People know it is bogus, but they all want to see it.' It was nearly midday, and we decided to give it a miss. Instead, Jocelyne suggested a visit to the Ksara caves. 'In 1857 a fox chasing a chicken discovered the caves,' Jocelyne recounted. 'Then someone started chasing the fox and followed it into a cavity, and lo! there was this vast labyrinth of caves.' They turned out to be Roman wine cellars that had been abandoned and lost for centuries, a lair of wild animals now and bats. The Romans dug the cellars inside the mountains to ensure perfect maturing in a cool and steady temperature of 11–13°. The narrow paths, lit by naked bulbs, ran between rows of wine barrels which looked like huge brooding birds. Lamartine and Gérard de Nerval among others praised 'the golden wines of Ksara... the blessed beverage of the gods'. Jocelyne said that the Jesuit Fathers produce the wines, tending hundreds of hectares of vineyard. In the cellars' shop, a variety of bottles were set out. Being a teetotaller, I only bought three, presents for Jocelyne and my new Beirut friends. Being a Muslim, Salman did not want any.

The colossal columns of Baalbek loomed in the horizon as if they upheld the sky. An awe-inspiring sight – one might have been approaching the abode of the gods. And it has been so forever. Baalbek started as a temple to the Semitic sky-god Baal, who was also the 'Lord of the Land', the Bek, hence Baalbek. The Greek Seleucids who conquered the region identified him with their own Greek sun god Helios and called the place Heliopolis or 'City of the Sun'. By the time the

Romans arrived in 1st Century AD, little was left of those early shrines save the sacred acres, on which they built the temples whose remnants we see today. They named the city Julia Augusta Felix after the daughter of Octavius, later Augustus, for it was during his reign, in 16 BC, that the foundation stone of the Temple of Jupiter was laid. It was finished 76 years later in 60 AD, while the whole complex took over two hundred years to complete. Some historians assign the present Roman buildings' foundation to Antoninus Pius (86-161 AD), the dedication to Septimius Severus (193-211) and the completion to the reigns of Caracalla and Philip the Arab. The whole thing seems to have gone up in what Gibbon called the 'Age of Antoninus', the Empire's Golden Age.

At any rate, these were the grandest religious monuments in the antique world, and the gigantic scale of everything reflects the power of the Roman Empire at its apogee. As the Semitic gods were worshipped in triads – a god, a goddess and one of the cast of secondary deities – the Romans built three actual temples, and the largest was dedicated to Jupiter. For the sake of continuity, the Roman gods were identified with their previous avatars as Baal, Astarte and Adonis. When Constantine converted the Empire to Christianity and moved his capital to Constantinople, he suppressed the worship of those pagan gods. By the time of Emperor Theodosius (379-95), earthquakes had already damaged the Temple of Jupiter; he carried on the work by destroying the facade and courtyard and erecting a basilica. The Arabs arrived in 634, and thereafter Baalbek remained in Muslim hands. The Crusades, internecine conflicts, the Mongols in 1260 and finally Tamerlane in 1400 – not to mention many natural disasters – completed the ravages of time. Little of the original Baalbek was left standing. But popular legends sprang up around the ruins, and they persist to this day. Some say that Baalbek was built by Cain as an act of

contrition after his banishment by God; others believe that
Solomon, under the influence of his foreign wives, built it in
honour of Astarte.

The ruins were discovered by European travellers in the
16th Century, who alerted the West. The Reverend Henry
Maundrell, a chaplain to the Levant Company in Aleppo, wrote
in 1697: 'a noble ruin... the only curiosity for which this place
is wont to be visited'. Lady Hester Stanhope and Lamartine
were enthusiastic about its harmonious grandeur. In Gertrude
Bell's view it was 'second to none save the Temple group of
Athenian Acropolis'.

Excavation and restoration began in the 19th Century, and
what we see today is the result of the patient devotion of archaeologists and antiquarians ever since, in particular the work of
German and French teams since 1900.

We crossed the river and entered the dusty and crowded
Baalbek town and hastened to the ruins. During the civil war,
they were used as ammunition depots, and even today there are
Hezbollah strongholds in the surrounding hills; but now the
place seems peaceful. Outside the ruins, caparisoned camels
and donkeys were touted for rides for children and adults, and
photographers snapped them once mounted on the docile
animals. Stalls set up under trellises and trees were selling odds
and ends; the fumes of spicy, charcoal-grilled meat and sizzling
flafa drew sightseers to food stalls and kebab stands. I love
street food; whatever the quality of the ingredients, it always
tastes good and puts you in touch with local people. We bought
some flafa and shwarmas and ate them sitting on the steps at the
entrance of the ruins.

The temples were lifted on a wide stone dais high above the
surrounding country. The gateway, or propylae, is a flight of
monumental steps, a colonnaded portico with columns of red

granite from Aswan, and two towers, which were later turned into fortresses by the Arabs. This leads to a hexagonal court – apparently a shape unknown in Roman architecture – and further along to the vast courtyard of the Temple of Jupiter. Ornate porticoes surround it, with niches for statues; two pools, one on each side, contain carved nereids and cupids gambolling all round. Here Theodosius built a basilica and dedicated it to St Peter; eventually it was wrecked by a sequence of earthquakes. When the débris was cleared away so that archaeological work could begin, a sacrificial altar was laid bare. There on special days as many as a hundred bulls would have been led through underground passages and ritually killed by priests in gold and crimson robes, then cooked and distributed among the congregation.

At the far end of the courtyard rise the majestic columns of Jupiter's temple, with honey-coloured sunlight streaming down their time-polished surfaces. Only six of the original 54 columns remain, consisting of three drums each and measuring 65 feet, the largest in the world. Justinian took eight of them away for Hagia Sophia, and some lie broken on the ground, but the rest are unaccounted for. There was a gold statue of the god holding a whip, a thunderbolt and ears of corn, marking 'the united forms of Jupiter and the Sun', according to Macrobius; it was lost when Constantine converted Rome to Christianity. Above the capitals, fragments of frieze show the heads of lions and bulls looped together with garlands, while the cornice is decorated with acanthus leaves and egg-and-dart moulding – the symbols of life and death – and lions' heads whose open mouths spout water.

They say that there was once an oracle here which foretold the death of Emperor Trajan. Amid the mass of remnants on the ground is a bas-relief of Antony and Cleopatra – apparently Antony gave her Baalbek and Anjar as a present. It reminded me of Hafiz's lines:

If the Beloved deigns to accept my heart,
For her dark beauty I shall give away Samarkand and Bokhara.

What are a couple of great cities when the stake is love itself? Only the profligacy of emperors and poets can measure up to the generosity of love.

We moved on to the Temple of Bacchus, so called because of its carvings of the god and of vine leaves and grapes. Originally it was dedicated to Astarte/Venus, and it is distinguished by its exquisite proportions, its fluted Sienna-coloured columns and the exuberance of its decoration. In spite of repeated calamities – in particular the earthquake of 1759, which dislodged the keystone and threatened the collapse of the whole edifice – it is the best preserved Roman temple in the world. *O, absit omen!*

The pretty, domed Temple of Venus takes its name from the fading figure of the goddess in the cella, rising in a shell from the sea, *Anayomene*, anticipating Botticelli. When Constantine forbade the cult of Venus, the temple became a church dedicated to Santa Barbara and eventually fell into serious disrepair. Yet it inspired Borromini for St Ivo in Rome, and Henry Hoare copied it at Stourhead. But the goddess cannot be denied with impunity, and it occurred to me (as it has to others in recent centuries) that her banishment – and later that of Eros – was perhaps Christianity's biggest *faux pas*, for which Christendom has paid through the ages with pain and perversion.

Before the civil war, Baalbek was the setting for an international music festival. When the gunfire finally died away, the moving voice of Fairouz resounded through the Temple of Jupiter in a concert that marked the beginning of reconciliation. If peace prevails and the country is secure, the Baalbek Festival will regain its former importance, to the glory of music and the harmony of nations. *Inshallah!*

The Fountain of Adonis   141

A short distance from the ruins, Jocelyne led me to a quarry and showed me the largest stone in the world. Hajar al-Hubla is 69 feet long and weighs a thousand tons; it is a lonely leviathan slowly sinking into the earth. Perhaps being even larger than the giants in the Temple of Jupiter, it was too heavy to move. There are other vestiges of the past in Baalbek town itself – the remains of a Mameluke grand mosque, for instance, bits of Roman catacombs and an amphitheatre underneath the old Palmyra Hotel.

It was my last day, and I wanted to get to Anjar before darkness fell. It is 24 miles further on the Beirut-Damascus highway and only six miles from the Syrian frontier. On the way we passed stalls of ceramics with time-honoured designs, glazed in lustrous primary colours. Patched and dun-coloured tents of migrant workers dotted the plain with children and animals milling round them. 'They make much children, but no school for them. Same with Palestinian refugees.' Salman shook his head, indicating how poverty and despair are perpetuated through lack of education and social cohesion.

Anjar, the ancient Chalcis, was the capital of Ptolemy, the Egyptian king who was executed by Mark Antony for having sided with the Persians. He presented the conquered city to Cleopatra as a token of his love. Later Augustus gave it to Herod the Great, and after many years Claudius granted it to Herod Agrippa's brother, with the title of king. His queen was Berenice, who after his death became the mistress of her own brother. Little is known about Berenice, except that when Titus came to Syria to subdue the Jews, he fell in love with her, and for a while she became his consort in Rome. On these meagre crumbs of information Racine raised the sublime edifice of his great tragedy *Bérénice*. It is the only one of his tragedies in which the chief actors are not pitched against the gods or Fate but against *raison d'état*. In Racine's version, Berenice never reaches Rome, for upon hearing that he has been proclaimed emperor, Titus decides to leave her in Syria and return alone. The Romans would not accept her as queen; strife would break out if he tried to force the issue, so he chooses to sacrifice his own happiness to duty and renounce her. Racine was a Jansenist. His tragedies express the predicament of the soul faced with the choice between the world and eternal salvation. It was as if his career at the court of the Sun King had confirmed his belief that there was no compatibility between the two. How and why we choose one or the other is determined by Grace, which is a mystery. Thus *his* Titus and Bérénice join the doomed lovers of myth and history: Tristan and Isolde, Antony and Cleopatra, Leyla and Majnoon…

I loved Racine's play when I first read it as a teenager and still remember some of the verses, which I learnt by heart – surely among the most beautiful in the French language. Now as we approached Anjar, the heartbreaking farewell scene between the lovers came to my mind:

> *Dans un mois, dans un an, comment soufrirons nous,*
> *Seigneur, que tant de mers me separent de vous?*
> *Que le jour recommence et que le jour finisse,*
> *Sans que jamais Titus puisse voir Bérénice,*
> *Sans que de tout le jour je puisse voir Titus…*

Modern Anjar was built by the Armenians who fled Turkey during the massacres of 1915-19 and took refuge in Lebanon. In three years, over two million Armenians were slaughtered – the first genocide, or 'ethnic cleansing', of the 20th Century and prototype of many that followed. 'After all, who remembers the murder of Armenians by Turks now?' Hitler is said to have remarked, when he was planning the Final Solution.

But I had come to see the remains of the 7th Century

Umayyad town, a mile south of the village. Excavated and partly restored, it is one of the few substantial vestiges of the Umayyad period. Beneath the veneer of their new faith of Islam, the Umayyads were desert Bedouins with pagan souls. Having no truck with religious austerity, they built themselves splendid palaces in gardens like Eden. There wine flowed, music played and at night women danced until the cry of muezzin ushered in the dawn. The Abbassids who succeeded the Umayyads accused them of heresy and tried to obliterate their memory by destroying their monuments. What remained was razed to the ground by the invading Mongols and, later, Tamerlane. The Great Mosque in Damascus survived by a solitary miracle; but to see the full decorative splendour of Umayyad architecture one has to go to Andalusia – to Granada, Cordoba and Seville.

It is believed that Anjar was mostly built by Khalif Walid I over the ruins of the Roman Chalcis, following its rectangular layout and using some of the surviving materials. The town stood on high ground cooled by mountain breezes on the caravan route from Damascus to the sea. It commanded magnificent views over the Bekaa Valley. Stone walls encircled it, punctuated with forty round towers and a gate at either side. The two colonnaded main roads – cardo maximus and decumanus – were flanked by six hundred shops, and where they crossed stood a tetrapylon. The town was Walid's summer capital, and away from the commercial centre he built himself an elegant palace on two floors with a central court in the Byzantine style. There are the remains of a smaller palace, doubtless the harem, and of a mosque and a hammam with mosaic paving. To classical grandeur, the Khalif's architects added Oriental refinements: porticoes of slender columns, enticing archways and carvings like embroidery in stone. The result was a town whose beauty and harmony still seem to compose the spirit and soothe the soul.

We reached Anjar just before sunset and drove straight to the ruined city. Not a soul was in sight, only a caretaker at the gate, who said we were his only visitors that day. 'Hundreds of cars and coaches on the road, but they don't stop here,' he lamented. I was delighted and, leaving my companions with him, took a walk by myself. A gentle melancholy born of silence and oblivion pervaded the place. Here and there a tuft of grass sprang up between stones; a pair of white butterflies balanced on a blade; a troop of ants were marching to their mysterious goal. As the sun went down, I headed back towards the gate and sat in the shade of a pine grove to gaze down along the sweep and splendour of the valley. Then I joined my companions.

We said goodbye to the guardian and drove a mile to the only restaurant near the site. It was huge and empty, save for a few waiters looking listless. Counters in the middle bulged with dishes of mezes and raw vegetables, fish and meat, but for whom? Outside of the main room, a long empty pool under a marquee of vines and flowering creepers had collected fallen leaves. In the garden, dry leaves whirled in the evening breeze. We sat by the empty pool and ordered our meal. Presently, a wedding party arrived, and the place was instantly transformed. Lights came on; abundant food and drink appeared as if by conjuring; music and laughter filled the air; cameras clicked, and the bride and groom began to dance, followed by the guests. 'Come and join us! Come and dance!' they said as they twirled past our table. I marvelled at the fortitude and *joie-de-vivre* of the Lebanese; after eighteen years of fighting and devastation that would have broken the spirit of lesser people, they missed no opportunity to celebrate life.

Outside, the moon had risen over the forgotten city. I imagined a caravan of ghosts passing through Anjar and, hearing the sounds of merriment, pausing to look on – or was it perhaps only Titus and Berenice, strolling over from their palace to enjoy the revels and bless the newlyweds, hoping that unlike themselves these young lovers would never part?

Before leaving for the airport, I asked Salman to stop the car outside a bookshop, rushed in and bought two English-Arabic dictionaries for him and Jocelyne. 'For your birthdays' – they were soon to be 21 and 23. A few months later, I received a letter from Salman saying that he had managed to find the money and take an English course, as I had urged him to do. Indeed, his grammar and vocabulary seemed to have greatly improved. 'I will not forget you,' he wrote.

In the end, it is human encounters that make a landscape and a journey memorable. To me, the beautiful country of Aphrodite and Adonis is also the homeland of my two young companions. I will not forget them either.